EXPLORING THE TORAH

Temple Beth David
6100 Hefley Street
Westminster, CA 92683
(714) 892-6623

EXPLORING THE TORAH

By

SHIRLEY STERN

KTAV PUBLISHING HOUSE, INC.
HOBOKEN, NEW JERSEY

CONTENTS

BEFORE WE BEGIN

"When God first began to create the heavens and the earth, the earth was an unformed, dark mass." These words from the Torah begin the most dramatic story ever written—a story that begins with the creation of the world and ends with the entry of the Jewish people into the land we now know as Israel. The Torah tells the story in simple but vivid language. It traces the history of a nation which despite many trials and tribulations never lost faith in the God who had rescued its people from slavery and would deliver them as free men and women to the land of their ancestors.

The Torah, however, is more than just an exciting and dramatic story. It is the beginning of the sacred literature of Judaism. All later Jewish religious tradition is based on it. The Torah contains a code of laws that is not only the basis of Judaism but provides the ethical and legal framework for almost all the people of the civilized world. The Christians recognized the importance of the Torah by making it part of their Holy Scriptures (they called it the Old Testament and called their own additions the New Testament). Mohammed, the founder of the Moslem religion, called the Jewish people the "People of the Book" because the greatest book of all, the Torah, came from them.

You are about to begin your study of the Torah. *Exploring the Torah* was especially written to help you understand and appreciate this great heritage of ours. It is a translation of the Torah into modern English. Some of the biblical text is condensed to make it easier to understand and study, but large portions of narrative material, religious laws, and ethical and legal codes are included to give you the true "flavor" of the text. Also included with the text are biblical commentaries from ancient days to our own time. These commentaries help us to understand the words of the Torah and give us insights into how scholars and religious leaders in different periods of history understood the Torah.

I hope that you will enjoy studying *Exploring The Torah* and that it will enhance your understanding of our wonderful heritage.

SHIRLEY STERN

I

The Beginning

Genesis 1–6:8

*God creates the world and all that is in it in six days,
and seeing that all that was created is good, God rests
on the seventh day, Shabbat, and makes it holy.*

*But God soon realizes that although the world is good,
people aren't always good.*

Summary: GENESIS 1:1–31

When God first began to create the heavens and the earth, the
earth was an unformed, dark mass. God created light and darkness. The light was called Day and the darkness was called Night.
That was the first day of creation. On the second day God created
the sky. On the third day God separated the seas from the dry
land and created all plant life. On the fourth day the sun, the
moon, and the stars were created. On the fifth day God created all
the creatures of the sky and the water. On the sixth day all the animals were created. Then God made a person in His own image.
God created male and female—(the man Adam, and the woman
Eve). God blessed them and said, "Be fertile and reproduce, and
fill the earth with your offspring." God made human beings to
rule over all the other creatures.

And God saw	וַיַּרְא אֱלֹהִים
all that He had made and found	אֶת־כָּל־אֲשֶׁר עָשָׂה
that it was very good.	וְהִנֵּה־טוֹב מְאֹד
And it was evening and morn-ing,	וַיְהִי־בֹקֶר וַיְהִי־עֶרֶב
the sixth day.	יוֹם הַשִּׁשִּׁי

I

COMMENTARIES

From the Talmud

Everything that God created has value. Even animals and insects that seem useless, or deadly, at first sight have an important purpose to fulfill. The snail is a remedy for boils, the housefly is ground up to make a powder to cure hornet stings, the gnat is used as an antidote against the poison of a snake, and the lizard is an antidote against scorpion poisoning.

God had a very specific reason for creating human beings last of all the creatures. He wanted them to know that the whole world was ready and waiting for them, and that the rest of the world was created just for them. But God had another reason. He did not want human beings to become too arrogant, and so they must know that even the lowliest insect was created before they were.

From the Mishnah

God created a single human being so that all might be descended from one ancestor, and no one could say, "I am better than you because my ancestor was more important."

FOCUS ON: VALUES

The Talmud says that even the lowliest creatures have a purpose in the universe. Modern ecologists agree. Every form of life, no matter how small or insignificant, is important in the chain of life; and every species of life is dependent on other species for survival.

LEARNING MORE ABOUT:
BIBLICAL COMMENTARY

The Torah is the basic textbook of Judaism. It is the written foundation of Jewish law and learning. Throughout Jewish history rabbis and scholars searched for ways to explain the ideas in the Torah. They developed a system of commentaries and interpretations known as the Oral Law, so-called because for many centuries it was not written down, but memorized by the rabbis and passed on orally from generation to generation.

There are two types of commentary—Halacha and Aggada. The Halacha consists of laws—both religious and civil laws. The Aggada is made up of stories and folktales that communicate the spirit and feeling of Judaism.

Biblical commentary is contained in the Midrash, the Talmud, Rashi, and other commentaries. Interpretation of the Bible continues to this day as scholars strive to gain new insights and understanding.

Throughout this book we will annotate the Biblical passages with both traditional and modern commentaries. We will also explore (in these "LEARNING MORE ABOUT" sections) how various commentaries developed and who some of the commentators were.

FOCUS ON:
BIBLICAL SELECTIONS IN THE PRAYERBOOK

Although the prayerbook also contains prayers of more recent origin, many of its prayers are from the Torah. The Friday evening Kiddush, which is quoted from Genesis 2:1–3, is an example.

It was evening and it was morning	וַיְהִי־עֶרֶב וַיְהִי־בֹקֶר
on the sixth day.	יוֹם הַשִּׁשִּׁי:
The heavens, the earth and all that was in them were completed.	וַיְכֻלּוּ הַשָּׁמַיִם וְהָאָרֶץ וְכָל־צְבָאָם:
God finished on the seventh day	וַיְכַל אֱלֹהִים בַּיּוֹם הַשְּׁבִיעִי,
All the work which He had done.	מְלַאכְתּוֹ אֲשֶׁר עָשָׂה:
And He rested on the seventh day	וַיִּשְׁבֹּת בַּיּוֹם הַשְּׁבִיעִי
from all the work that He had done.	מִכָּל מְלַאכְתּוֹ אֲשֶׁר עָשָׂה:
And God blessed the seventh day	וַיְבָרֶךְ אֱלֹהִים אֶת יוֹם הַשְּׁבִיעִי
and made it holy,	וַיְקַדֵּשׁ אֹתוֹ,
Because on it God had rested	כִּי בוֹ שָׁבַת מִכָּל מְלַאכְתּוֹ
from all the work,	
Which God in creating had done.	אֲשֶׁר בָּרָא אֱלֹהִים לַעֲשׂוֹת:

4

Summary: GENESIS 2:1–3

On the sixth day God completed the heavens and the earth and all the living things that inhabited them.

And God rested on the seventh day	וַיִּשְׁבֹּת בַּיּוֹם הַשְּׁבִיעִי
from all the work	מִכָּל־מְלַאכְתּוֹ
that He had done.	אֲשֶׁר עָשָׂה:

COMMENTARIES

From the Midrash

God worked very hard for six days to create the world. When He finished, the world was almost perfect. It lacked only one thing, "Rest." So for the seventh day, Shabbat, God created rest.

From the Zohar

Before God created the heavens and the earth there was no one to praise Him and tell of His glory. Then God created the angels and humans, who were to praise God. But during the week of creation there was no time to proclaim God's glory. Only on Shabbat, when all creation rested, did all the beings on earth and in heaven break into songs of adoration.

SOMETHING TO THINK ABOUT

Scholars believe that the idea of a seven-day week with a day of rest on the last day is a Jewish invention. How would the world be different if this concept had never been invented? How would *your* life be different?

Adam and Eve lived in the Garden of Eden. In the Garden grew every tree that was beautiful to look at and good to eat. In the center of the Garden were the Tree of Life and the Tree of Knowledge.

God said, "Of every tree in the Garden you may eat, but not of the Tree of Knowledge, for if you do, you will die."

But the serpent, the shrewdest of all wild beasts, tricked the woman, and she ate of the fruit of the tree and gave some to her husband, and he also ate of it.

Because of this, God punished the man and the woman and drove them out of the Garden of Eden. To Adam God said,

"By the sweat of your brow	בְּזֵעַת אַפֶּיךָ
you will get bread to eat	תֹּאכַל לֶחֶם
until you return to the ground,	עַד שׁוּבְךָ אֶל־הָאֲדָמָה
for you were taken from the ground.	כִּי מִמֶּנָּה לֻקָּחְתָּ
For dust you are,	כִּי־עָפָר אַתָּה
and to dust you will return."	וְאֶל־עָפָר תָּשׁוּב:

6

COMMENTARIES

From the Talmud

In the Garden of Eden the sun always shone and it was always beautiful. When Adam and Eve left the garden they experienced the setting of the sun and the approach of darkness for the first time. They wept in fear and shame because they believed that this was part of their punishment for disobeying God. But when morning came, they understood that this was the course of nature, and that day always follows the darkness of night. They rejoiced, and Adam sacrificed an offering to God.

From Rashi

Adam was created from the dust of the four corners of the world, so that wherever human beings die, the earth will accept them in burial.

FOCUS ON: VALUES

Eve sinned and ate the fruit of the Tree of Knowledge because she was tricked by the serpent. Adam sinned because he was persuaded by Eve.

Sometimes we let ourselves be led or persuaded by others to do something wrong. To what extent are we accountable when we allow ourselves to be passive participants in wrongdoing?

SOMETHING TO THINK ABOUT

Jews use the term "Tree of Life" to refer to the Torah. In what way does the Torah give everlasting life to the Jews?

Adam and Eve had two sons, Cain and Abel. Cain was a farmer, and Abel was a shepherd.

One day the two brothers brought offerings to God. Abel brought a lamb from his flock, and Cain brought of the fruit of the ground. God favored Abel's offering, but did not accept Cain's. This made Cain very angry, and he killed his brother Abel.

God called to Cain and asked, "Where is your brother Cain?"

Cain answered, "I do not know.	וַיֹּאמֶר לֹא יָדַעְתִּי
Am I my brother's keeper?"	הֲשֹׁמֵר אָחִי אָנֹכִי:

God said, "What have you done? Your brother's blood cries out to Me from the ground." God punished Cain. He drove him from his home and caused him to be a homeless wanderer on the earth. But God put a mark on Cain so that no one would harm him.

Many years passed. Adam and Eve became the parents of another son, Seth. Adam and Eve's children became parents and they had children who had children of their own. People began to multiply on the face of the earth.

Adam's son Seth became the father of Enosh, who became the father of Kenan, who became the father of Mahalalel, who became the father of Jared, who became the father of Enoch, who fathered Methuselah, who was Lamech's father. Lamech had a son and he called him Noah. When Noah lived to be 500 years old he had three sons, Shem, Ham, and Japheth.

COMMENTARIES

From the Midrash

Abel was physically stronger than Cain. As the two brothers fought in the field, Abel overcame Cain. He would have been the winner. But Cain begged for mercy. Abel, who was kind and gentle, released his hold on Cain. As soon as Cain was free, he turned once again on Abel and killed him. Therefore wise people say, "Do not be good to those who are evil, or evil will befall you."

From the Mishnah

When God called to Cain and said, "Your brother's blood cries out to Me," He used the plural form for blood (that is, "bloods"). This is to teach us that not only Abel called out to God, but also all of Abel's descendants who would now never be born.

SOMETHING TO THINK ABOUT

When God asks Cain, "Where is your brother Abel?" Cain answers, "Am I my brother's keeper?" Do you think we are our brothers' keepers? That is, do you think that human beings are responsible for one another? To what extent? Why do you think so?

LEARNING MORE ABOUT:
THE CYCLE OF TORAH READINGS

It is a practice among Jews all over the world to read a special portion of the Torah each week. The Torah is divided into sections. Each section is called a *Sidra*. There are just enough Sidrot to complete the reading of the Torah in one year. Every synagogue, no matter where in the world it is located, reads the same Sidra on any given Shabbat.

The cycle of Torah readings begins on the Shabbat after Simchat Torah with the reading of the Sidra *Beresheet*. It ends on Simchat Torah with the reading of the Sidra *Vezot Habracha*.

In addition to the Sidra, a portion from the Prophets is also read. This is called the Haftarah. Generally, the Haftarah portion has some relationship to the Sidra.

The Torah and Haftarah are chanted with special musical notes called "Trope." Since it requires a great deal of training to master this way of reading, only a few Jews have the necessary expertise to read the Torah for the congregation. But all Jews can participate in the Torah reading by being called up to the Torah to recite the blessings before and after the reading. This is called "receiving an aliyah."

Being called to the Torah for an aliyah is considered a great honor. Usually, boys and girls who are Bar or Bat Mitzvah are given this honor.

THE TROPE SIGNS

פָּזֵר	זַרְקָא	מֵרְכָא
קַדְמָא	סֶגֹּל	טִפְחָא
וְאַזְלָא	דַּרְגָּא	מֻנַּח
תְּלִישָׁא־קְטַנָּה	תְּבִיר	אֶתְנַחְתָּא
תְּלִישָׁא־גְדוֹלָה	רְבִיעִי	מַהְפַּךְ
פְּסִיק	זָקֵף־גָּדוֹל	פַּשְׁטָא
סוֹף־פָּסוּק :	גֵּרְשַׁיִם	מֻנַּח
	יְתִיב	קָטֹן

II

Noah

Genesis 6:9–10:32

The world becomes corrupt and evil, and God decides to put an end to all life by causing a flood to cover the earth. But Noah, a righteous person in his generation, is saved, along with his family and animals of every kind, so that the earth may again be replenished with living beings.

After the waters have receded, God makes a covenant with Noah promising that He will never again destroy all life on earth.

Summary: GENESIS 6:9–7:5

Noah was a righteous man in his generation who walked with God. But the rest of the world was corrupt and evil. God said to Noah, "I have decided to destroy the earth and all the creatures in it. But I will save you. Build for yourself an ark of gopher wood, and cover it inside and out with pitch. Then enter the ark with your wife, your sons, and your sons' wives. Also take into the ark with you a male and female of every animal, bird, and insect on earth. I am about to bring a flood which will destroy all life on earth."

And Noah did	וַיַּעַשׂ נֹחַ
as God commanded him to do.	כְּכֹל אֲשֶׁר־צִוָּהוּ יְהוָה

COMMENTARIES

From Rashi

The Torah says that Noah was a righteous person in his generation. Some of the commentators believe this to mean that had Noah lived in a generation of righteous people, he would have been even more righteous. But other commentators explain it to Noah's discredit. In comparison to his own generation he was considered righteous. But had he lived in the generation of Abraham, he would not have been considered of any importance.

From the Talmud

Noah was saved from destruction because he was a "righteous person in his generation." We learn from this that everyone else in Noah's generation was evil.

Noah was worthy of special praise because it is especially difficult to be honest and good when everyone else is dishonest and evil.

From the Midrash

In the years before the flood people lived under ideal conditions. They were prosperous without having to work hard for what they had. When they planted seeds in their fields, enough grain grew to feed them for forty years without replanting. Because things were so easy for them, they became lazy and arrogant. Soon they were so evil that they rebelled against God. It was for this reason that they were destroyed.

SOMETHING TO THINK ABOUT

According to the Midrash, the evils of the world in Noah's day came from people having things too easy. We live in a world where everything is much easier for us than it was for people long ago. Our homes are heated and we don't have to chop wood for a fire. Our food comes to us neatly packaged from the supermarket shelf and we don't have to catch it or grow it ourselves. We have instant entertainment on television, and quick, easy transportation anywhere in the world.

Do you think that this way of life makes us lazy, arrogant, dishonest, or evil? Why do you think so?

God commanded Noah to build an ark so that his neighbors would see him working on it and ask what it was for. God hoped that when the people realized what would happen to them because of their wicked ways, they would repent and change their behavior. But the people paid no attention to Noah and what he was doing, and as a result, they all died in the flood.

In the 600th year of Noah's life it began to rain and the flood came. Noah and his wife, and his sons and his sons' wives entered the ark, along with a male and female of every kind of living creature that lived on earth.

The flood continued	וַיְהִי הַמַּבּוּל
for forty days on the earth.	אַרְבָּעִים יוֹם עַל־הָאָרֶץ.

    The water raised the ark so that it rose above the earth. And the ark drifted upon the water. Soon the water covered even the highest mountain. All life on earth that was not in the ark perished—birds, cattle, beasts, insects, and all mankind. All existence on earth was blotted out. Only Noah and those with him in the ark were left.

COMMENTARIES

From the Midrash

Noah's neighbors watched him build the ark and they laughed. They did not believe that there would really be a flood that would kill all life on earth.

    But when it began to rain very hard, and it looked like there would really be a flood, the people were afraid. They came to Noah and said, "Please let us join you on the ark."

    But Noah did not allow them to enter the ark. "Aren't you the same people who said there is no God and there would be no flood," he asked. "And now you want God's protection. God will not help you. You may not enter the ark."

    The people pleaded with Noah. "We are sorry," they said. "We will repent and be good."

    But Noah continued to guard the entrance to the ark. "It took me a long time to build the ark," he said. "You could have repented while I was building it, and God would have saved you. But you did not. Now you are ready to repent because you know that you will die. God will not listen to you now. You must die in the waters of the flood."

Summary: GENESIS 7:24–8:14

When the waters had swelled on the earth for 150 days, God remembered Noah and all the beasts and cattle that were with him in the ark. And God caused a wind to blow across the earth, and the waters subsided. The waters continued to recede steadily from the earth.

The ark came to rest	וַתָּנַח הַתֵּבָה
in the seventh month,	בַּחֹדֶשׁ הַשְּׁבִיעִי
on the seventeenth day of the month,	בְּשִׁבְעָה־עָשָׂר יוֹם לַחֹדֶשׁ
on Mount Ararat.	עַל הָרֵי אֲרָרָט:

Soon the tops of all the mountains were visible. At the end of forty days Noah opened one of the windows of the ark and sent out a raven. It flew around until the waters dried up and did not return to the ark. Then Noah sent out a dove, but it returned because it could find no resting place. After seven days had passed, Noah sent the dove out once more. It returned with an olive leaf in its beak. Then Noah knew that the waters had receded. He waited another seven days and again sent the dove from the ark. This time it did not return. The earth was dry.

COMMENTARIES

From the Midrash

In addition to the people and animals in the ark, some very unusual beings also sought refuge. One of these was "Falsehood." It came to Noah when he was building the ark and asked to be allowed to come aboard.

"You must have a partner," said Noah. "No one can come on the ark without a mate."

So "Falsehood" approached "Misfortune," who agreed to accompany him on the ark. And together the pair survived the flood.

That is why throughout time, and even in our own day, "Falsehood" is always accompanied by "Misfortune."

FOCUS ON VALUES

The commentary you just read makes the point that falsehood is always accompanied by misfortune. This means that bad things will happen to you if you lie. Do you think this is so? Think of a situation in your own life when this was true. Do you think a lie is ever justified? When?

Discuss this with your parents and see how they feel about it.

Noah came out of the ark. With him were his wife, his sons, and his sons' wives. Every animal, every creeping thing, and every living thing that stirs on earth came out of the ark with their families.

Noah thanked God. He built an altar and offered on it burnt offerings to God. God smelled the pleasing aroma and said to Himself: "I will never again doom the world and destroy every living being in it as I have done." God blessed Noah and his family and said, "Be fertile and increase and fill the earth."

God said to Noah and his sons, "I now establish My covenant with you and with every living thing that is with you—with all the birds, cattle, and wild beasts.

I will make a covenant with you:	וַהֲקִמֹתִי־אֶת בְּרִיתִי אִתְּכֶם
Never again shall all living things be destroyed	וְלֹא־יִכָּרֵת כָּל־בָּשָׂר עוֹד
by a flood,	מִמֵּי הַמַּבּוּל
and never again shall there be a flood to	וְלֹא־יִהְיֶה עוֹד מַבּוּל
destroy the earth."	לְשַׁחֵת הָאָרֶץ:

And God set His rainbow in the sky as a sign of the covenant between Him and all living beings that there would never again be a flood to destroy all life.

COMMENTARIES

From the Midrash

After the water had receded from the earth, Noah did not immediately leave the ark. He did not step out on dry land even after God had commanded him to do so. He stayed in the ark, where he felt safe and secure.

When God commanded him a second time to leave, he said, "I am afraid to leave. Suppose I go back to my home and then become the father of more children. Suppose those children grow up and are wicked. Suppose God wants to destroy the earth once more. It is better if I remain in the ark and do not return to my home."

But God wanted Noah to return to his home, and so He promised that the earth would never again be destroyed by a flood. Then Noah left the ark and returned to his home.

From the Zohar

When Noah left the ark and stepped on dry land, he looked all around him. Wherever he looked there was destruction and desolation from the waters of the flood. Noah was very sad, and he called out to God, "O Lord, what have you done? You call yourself a God of mercy, but you did not show any mercy for the creatures of the world whom you destroyed."

God heard Noah's words and answered, "Noah, you are a foolish man. When I told you there would be a flood, you did not object. When I told you that all living things would die in it, you did not object. When I told you to build an ark so that only you would be saved, you still did not object. Now that the earth has been destroyed and all living beings who were not in the ark have died, you object. Where were you when you could have spoken and saved the world?"

LEARNING MORE ABOUT:
STORIES OF A GREAT FLOOD

The story of Noah is a story about a great flood that destroyed the world. The story in the Bible is not the only story of a great flood. Somewhat similar stories are found in the folklore of many nations. Scientists believe that many thousands of years ago such a great flood actually took place and stories about it were handed down from generation to generation.

The story of a great flood that is most like the story in the Torah is the Babylonian story. It is found in a poem called the "Gilgamesh Epic." In that story all the gods decide to send a flood on the earth. One of the gods, Ea, decides to save his favorite human, Utnapishtim. Ea warns Utnapishtim and commands him to build a ship. When the ship is built, Utnapishtim fills it with his possessions, the members of his family, and domestic and wild animals. It rains for six days and nights. On the seventh day Utnapishtim sends out a dove, which returns to the ship. Later he sends out a raven, which does not return. All the people and animals in the ship then leave, and Utnapishtim offers a sacrifice to Ea.

Although many elements of the Gilgamesh story are similar to the story in the Bible, there are also many differences. The most important difference is that Noah was saved because he was good and worthy of being saved, while Utnapishtim was saved because the god was playing favorites.

FOCUS ON VALUES:

The story of Noah provides us with the first known lesson in ecology. It tells us that Noah took a male and a female of every living thing into the ark so that after the flood every species could reproduce and live on the earth once more.

Every species was important to God—even the lowliest were saved.

Modern ecologists would agree that every species is important. Every species has its purpose in the chain of life. Allowing any species, even the lowliest, to die out might affect other species in the chain, and in the end, even mankind might be affected.

III

The Tower of Babel

Genesis 11:1–32

People plan to build a city and a tower that reach to the sky. But God disapproves and confuses their languages so that they can no longer communicate with each other.

After many generations Abram, the son of Terach, is born. When Abram grows up, he and his wife, Sarai, go with Terach to live in Haran.

Summary: GENESIS 11:1–4

All the earth had the same language. As people migrated from the east, they came to a valley in the land of Shinar and settled there. They said to each other, "Let us make some bricks and burn them until they are hard." Then they said,

"Come, let us build a city	הָבָה נִבְנֶה־לָּנוּ עִיר
and a tower with its top in the sky	וּמִגְדָּל וְרֹאשׁוֹ בַשָּׁמַיִם
so that we will make a name for ourselves."	וְנַעֲשֶׂה לָּנוּ שֵׁם.

20

COMMENTARIES

From the Midrash

The tower got higher and higher. Many years passed. Soon the tower was so high that it took a year to climb to the top. The people building the tower became more and more eager to build their tower higher and higher. Soon the bricks they were using became more precious to them than human life. If a person fell down while he was working, they took no notice of it. But if a brick fell down from the top, they wept, because it would take a year to climb to the top and replace it.

SOMETHING TO THINK ABOUT

The builders of the tower were so involved in what they were doing that it became the most important thing in the world to them, and they ignored human values.

Have you ever become so absorbed in a project that you were irritable and impatient with those around you (or behaved badly in other ways)? How can people control this tendency? What can you do to control it in yourself?

God came down to look at the city and the tower that the people had built. God said, "If as one people with one language they act like this, then nothing will be out of their reach.

Let Me go down	הָבָה נֵרְדָה
and confuse their speech	וְנָבְלָה שָׁם שְׂפָתָם
so that they will not under-stand	אֲשֶׁר לֹא יִשְׁמְעוּ אִישׁ
one another's speech."	שְׂפַת רֵעֵהוּ.

Then God scattered the people over the face of the whole earth, and they stopped building the city. That is why it was called "Babel," because there the Lord confused their speech and scattered them all over the world.

COMMENTARIES

From the Midrash

The Torah says that God Himself came down to look at the city and the tower that the people had built. He came down to see for Himself before making a judgment. This is a lesson to human judges that they must personally examine the accused and know all the facts before they render a verdict.

Summary: GENESIS 11:10–32
This is the line of Shem, the son of Noah. Shem lived 500 years and was the father of sons and daughters. Shem was the father of Arpachshad. Arpachshad was the father of Shelah, who was the father of Eber. Eber was the father of Peleg, who was the father of Reu, who was the father of Serug. Serug was the father of Nahor, who was the father of Terach. Terach was seventy years old when he became the father of Abram.

Sarai became the wife of Abram and they had no children. Terach took his son Abram, his grandson Lot, the son of Abram's brother Haran, and his daughter-in-law Sarai, and they set out together for the land of Canaan;

but when they came as far as Haran,	וַיָּבֹאוּ עַד־חָרָן
they settled there.	וַיֵּשְׁבוּ שָׁם.

COMMENTARIES

From the Midrash

When Abram (later changed by God to Abraham) was still young, he discovered God. Although he was very young he got out of his cradle and walked about. Soon it was night. Abram looked up and saw the stars in the sky. They were very beautiful. "Those are the gods," he said. All night he looked up at them and admired their beauty.

Then dawn came. The stars disappeared from the sky. "I will not worship them," said Abram. "They disappear in the morning. They cannot be the gods." After a while the sun came out. It was very bright and it lit up the sky.

"This is God," said Abram. "I will worship the sun." But at the end of the day the sun, too, disappeared. "That is not God," said Abram.

When night came the moon appeared. Abram worshipped the moon. But it, too, disappeared in the morning.

The baby Abram thought and thought. "There is only one God," he said. "The only true God is the one who put the stars, sun, and moon into motion."

From that time forth Abram worshipped the one true God.

LEARNING MORE ABOUT BIBLICAL COMMENTARIES:
THE MIDRASH

Many of the Biblical commentaries that you have been reading are from the Midrash. Most of the Midrashic commentaries are in story form. These are called "Midrashim." The Midrashim were originally teaching texts. Our ancient rabbis were teachers. They wanted Jews to understand the meaning of passages in the Bible and to appreciate their value. The purpose of the Midrashic stories was to clarify and explain portions of the Bible that the ancient rabbis felt needed explanation.

The Midrash developed over a period of many hundreds of years, beginning quite early in Jewish history. At first the stories were handed down from generation to generation by word of mouth. They were part of what was called the "Oral tradition." But after a while scholars began to collect the Midrashim and publish them in volumes. Collections of Midrashim began to appear in Talmudic times and continued into the Middle Ages.

When reading these Midrashic stories, it is important to remember that their main purpose is to teach a lesson. Usually there will be a moral that is very clear and easy to understand. But sometimes the point of the story may be harder to find. When that is so, try to remember that the stories were written many years ago, and that sometimes people long ago understood things differently from the way we do today.

FOCUS ON VALUES:

The Midrash observes that the generation of the flood was destroyed entirely, while the generation of the Tower of Babel was not—it only had its languages confused. The rabbis asked, "Why were the people at the time of the flood worse than the people at the time of the Tower of Babel?" Their conclusion was that when the Tower was being built, the people were working together for one purpose. So important is peace and harmony to God that He was willing to spare their lives because they worked together harmoniously for a common goal.

IV

God Chooses Abraham

Genesis 12:1–17:27

God calls Abram and tells him to go to a land which will one day belong to his descendants. Abram and his wife, Sarai, and his nephew Lot leave their home. After a series of adventures they arrive in Canaan, the land promised by God.

Abram and Sarai are renamed Abraham and Sarah, and God promises that Sarah, who is very old and has no children, will have a child, Isaac, and that he will become the father of a great nation.

Summary: GENESIS 12:1–9

God said to Abram, "Go forth from your land and from your parents' house to the land that I will show you.

I will make you a great nation,	וְאֶעֶשְׂךָ לְגוֹי גָּדוֹל
and I will bless you.	וַאֲבָרֶכְךָ
I will make your name great,	וַאֲגַדְּלָה שְׁמֶךָ
and you shall be a blessing.	וֶהְיֵה בְּרָכָה:
I will bless those who bless you,	וַאֲבָרְכָה מְבָרְכֶיךָ
and I will curse those that curse you."	וּמְקַלֶּלְךָ אָאֹר

Abram went forth as God commanded him. His nephew Lot and his wife, Sarai, went with him, and they set out for Canaan.

When they came to Shechem, the Canaanites were in the land. God said, "I will give this land to your offspring."

Abram built an altar to God, who had appeared before him, and then continued on his way.

25

COMMENTARIES

From the Midrash

Even when Abraham was very young he did not believe in idols. Abram's father owned an idol shop. He would make idols and sell them to people who worshipped them. One day, Abram's father had to leave for a while. He put Abram in charge of the idol shop.

Abram wanted to show his father how foolish it was to worship idols of stone and wood. He thought of a plan. After his father had left, he smashed all but one of the idols, only leaving the very largest unharmed. Then he put a big stick in the hands of the remaining idol and a bowl of food in front of it.

When Terach, Abram's father, returned, he saw all the broken idols.

"What happened, Abram?" he asked.

Abram answered, "O my father, after you left I brought a bowl of food for the idols. The idols began to quarrel about who would get the food. But the largest idol would let none of the others near it. He took a big stick and broke all the other idols and took the food for himself."

Terach was angry. He knew that Abram was mocking him.

When Abram left his home to go to the land that God had promised to give to him, he did not know which land he was going to. He passed through several countries before he came to Canaan. In each one the inhabitants were behaving in ways that Abram did not approve of. They were drunk and lazy. "I hope that this is not the land that God promised," he said to himself.

But when Abram came to Canaan he saw that the people were industriously cultivating the land. "I hope that this is the land that God promised," he thought to himself.

Then God spoke to him and said, "To your descendants will I give this land."

Summary: GENESIS 12:10–13:18

There was a famine in the land of Canaan, and Abram and Sarai went to Egypt for food. Before they arrived in Egypt, Abram said to Sarai, "Pretend that you are my sister. If they know that you are my wife, they will kill me but let you live because you are so beautiful."

When Pharaoh's courtiers saw Sarai, they took her to the palace, and because of her it went well for Abram. He was given sheep and camels.

After Abram and Sarai left Egypt, they and Lot went to the Negev. Abram was very rich. He had cattle, silver, and gold. Lot also had flocks of sheep and herds of cattle. So vast were their possessions that the land could not hold them both. Abram's shepherds and Lot's shepherds began to quarrel.

Abram said to Lot,	וַיֹּאמֶר אַבְרָם אֶל־לוֹט
"Let there be no quarrel between you and me	אַל־נָא תְהִי מְרִיבָה בֵּינִי וּבֵינֶךָ
and between your shepherds and mine,	וּבֵין רֹעַי וּבֵין רֹעֶיךָ
for we are relatives.	כִּי־אֲנָשִׁים אַחִים אֲנָחְנוּ.

"Let us separate. If you go north, I will go south, and if you go south, I will go north."

Lot looked about him and saw that the Jordan Valley was fertile, and he chose the entire Jordan Valley.

Abram and Lot parted from each other, and Lot settled near Sodom, where the people were very wicked. When Lot had gone, God said to Abram, "Look about you on the north, south, east, and west. I will give this land to your descendants forever, and your descendants shall be as many as the dust of the earth."

And Abram moved his tent and came to live at Aylonai Mamre in Hebron, and there he built an altar to the Lord.

27

COMMENTARIES

From the Midrash

The famine in the time of Abram affected only the land of Canaan. God had caused the famine there in order to test Abram's faith. But Abram's faith in God was strong. He did not complain, nor was he impatient with God, who had commanded him to abandon his native land for a land of starvation.

From the Zohar

Abram should not have traveled to Egypt for food. He should have stayed in Canaan and had faith that God would provide food. Because of Abram's sin in leaving Canaan and going to Egypt, his descendants many years later were enslaved in Egypt. This was Abram's punishment for not having enough faith in God.

From the Talmud

Abraham should be praised for going to Egypt when there was no food in Canaan. From his action we learn that when there is a famine in a city, we should move away from that city as quickly as possible.

It happened that a war broke out between the kings of Shinar, Ellasar, Elam, and Goiim against the kings of Sodom, Gomorrah, Admah, Zeboiim, and Bela—four kings against five. The invaders seized all the wealth of Sodom and Gomorrah and went their way. They also took Lot, the son of Abram's brother, and his possessions, for he had settled in Sodom.

A fugitive brought the news of Lot's capture to Abram the Hebrew, who lived at Aylonai Mamre.

When Abram heard that his nephew had been taken captive, he took his servants, went in pursuit of the captors, and defeated them. He brought back all the possessions and his nephew Lot.

When Abram returned, the king of Sodom came out to meet him in the Valley of Shaveh, which is the Valley of the King. Melchizedek, the king of Salem, brought out bread and wine and blessed Abram and said,

"Blessed be Abram of God Most High,	בָּרוּךְ אַבְרָם לְאֵל עֶלְיוֹן
Creator of heaven and earth,	קֹנֵה שָׁמַיִם וָאָרֶץ:
and blessed be God Most High,	וּבָרוּךְ אֵל עֶלְיוֹן
who delivered your enemies into your hand."	אֲשֶׁר־מִגֵּן צָרֶיךָ בְּיָדֶךָ

29

COMMENTARIES

From the Midrash

Abram in this section is called Abram the Hebrew (Avram HaIvri). The word *Ivri* comes from the word *eyver* (עבר), meaning "on the other side of" or "beyond." From this we learn that the whole world was on one side and Abram was on the other—that is, Abram's faith was against what all other people believed.

Abram and his nephew Lot had not always gotten along too well, but when Abram heard that Lot had been captured, he forgot any quarrels he might have had with him and only considered how he might save him.

Sometime later the word of God came to Abram in a vision saying, "Do not be afraid, Abram. I am your shield. Your reward will be great. Count the stars in heaven if you are able to. So shall be your descendants.

I give this land to your off-spring,	לְזַרְעֲךָ נָתַתִּי אֶת־הָאָרֶץ הַזֹּאת
from the river of Egypt	מִנְּהַר מִצְרַיִם
to the great river, the Euphrates."	עַד הַנָּהָר הַגָּדֹל נְהַר־פְּרָת:

Sarai, Abram's wife, did not have any children. She had an Egyptian maid named Hagar whom she gave as a wife to Abram so that Abram might have children. Hagar and Abram became the parents of a son, Ishmael. Abram was eighty-six years old when Ishmael was born.

When Abram was ninety-nine years old, God appeared to him and said, "I am El Shaddai. Walk in My ways and I will establish My covenant with you, and you shall be the father of many nations. You shall no longer be called Abram, but your name shall be Abraham, for I make you the father of many nations. And I will keep My covenant with you and your descendants to come as an everlasting covenant through the ages. I give this land of Canaan to you and to your descendants as an everlasting possession. As a sign of the covenant between Me and you and your descendants, you shall circumcise every male child."

Then God said, "Your wife's name shall no longer be Sarai, but Sarah, and I will bless her and she will give birth to a son."

Abraham laughed and said to himself, "I am one hundred years old and Sarah is ninety. Can it be possible that we will become the parents of a child?"

31

And God said, "You will have a son and name him Isaac, and I will keep My covenant with him and his offspring. I will also bless Ishmael, and he, too, shall be the father of a great nation."

Then God was gone. Abraham circumcised himself and Ishmael and all the servants in his household.

LEARNING MORE ABOUT BIBLICAL COMMENTARIES: THE TALMUD

The Talmud is based on the teachings of the Bible. It interprets Biblical laws and commandments but also branches out into many other areas of knowledge. It contains historical information, scientific discussions, ethical teachings, legends, and practical wisdom. The subjects it covers include farming, prayer, medicine, astronomy, marriage and divorce, business matters, crime and punishment, government, and just about everything else you can think of.

The Talmud is composed of two basic divisions, the Mishnah and the Gemara. At first the Mishnah was an oral commentary on the Bible and was handed down by word of mouth. It was finally written down about 200 C.E. In the centuries that followed, new generations of rabbis studied the Mishnah. Their discussions were gathered together with the Mishnah in the Talmud.

There are actually two Talmuds, the Babylonian and the Jerusalem. The Babylonian Talmud is the better-known and contains the discussions of the rabbis of Babylonia. The Babylonian Talmud and the Jerusalem Talmud both include the same Mishnah.

The Talmud is made up of two different kinds of writings—Halacha and Aggada. Halacha is law. About two-thirds of the Talmud is law. Aggada is story. The Aggada is made up of legends, debates, wise sayings, and even humor. The Aggada was used by the scholars to make special points.

FOCUS ON VALUES:

The ritual of circumcision is very important. The Talmud requires that it take place exactly on the eighth day of birth, not a day before or after. However, when circumcising a boy on the eighth day would endanger the life of the child, the Talmud allows the child to be circumcised whenever it is medically safe to do so. The life of the child is more important than the strict performance of the ritual.

33

V

Sodom and Gomorrah

Genesis 18:1–21:34

Three "men" appear at Abraham's tent and tell him that Sarah will have a son. Sarah is doubtful and laughs. The "men" (really messengers of God) also tell Abraham that Sodom and Gomorrah will be destroyed because of the wickedness of their inhabitants. Abraham pleads for the cities, but they are destroyed, and only Lot and his family are saved.

Abraham and Sarah's long-awaited son, Isaac, is born, but problems arise between Abraham's two sons, Isaac and Ishmael, and Ishmael is sent away.

Summary: GENESIS 18:1–15

Abraham sat at the entrance to his tent in the heat of the day. He looked up and saw three men standing near him. As soon as he saw them, he ran to greet them. He brought water to bathe their feet and food to feed them.

The men said to him, "Where is your wife Sarah?" and he answered, "She is in the tent." Then one said, "Your wife Sarah shall have a son." Sarah was listening at the entrance of the tent, which was behind him,

and Sarah laughed to herself.   וַתִּצְחַק שָׂרָה בְּקִרְבָּהּ

The Lord then said to Abraham, "Why did Sarah laugh, saying, 'Shall I really have a child at my age?' Nothing is too miraculous for God. Sarah shall have a son."

34

COMMENTARIES

From the Midrash

Abraham was sitting at the entrance of his tent so that he might see any strangers who passed by and invite them in and offer them his hospitality.

One day Abraham invited a stranger into his tent. He offered him food and water and treated him with great kindness, as was his practice.

The stranger was very grateful. He expressed his gratitude to Abraham. He also prayed to his god of stone, thanking the god for his good fortune in having found Abraham's tent.

Abraham was very angry when he found the stranger praying to an idol, and he chased him out of his tent.

God saw what had happened and scolded Abraham, "I have put up with this man for many years, although he prayed to idols and did not worship Me. You could not even put up with him for one night."

Abraham was very sorry for what he had done. He ran after the stranger, found him, and brought him back to his tent, where he treated him with kindness and consideration.

The three men set out from Abraham's tent and looked toward Sodom. Then God said, "The wickedness of Sodom is very great. I will destroy Sodom."

Abraham came forward and said, "Will you destroy the innocent along with the guilty? What if there are fifty innocent people in the city? Will you not forgive the others for the sake of the fifty?"

God answered, "If I find fifty innocent people in Sodom, I will forgive the city."

Abraham spoke up saying, "What if there are five less than fifty? Will you destroy the whole city because there are five less?"

God answered, "I will not destroy it if I find forty-five."

Abraham spoke again and said, "Suppose there are only forty?"

God answered, "I will not do it if I find forty."

What if thirty should be found?" asked Abraham.

God answered, "I will not do it if I find thirty there."

"What if twenty should be found?" asked Abraham.

"I shall not do it for twenty," answered God.

"What if there are only ten?" asked Abraham.

"I will not destroy for the sake of ten," answered the Lord.

When God had finished talking to Abraham, He left. That evening two angels arrived in Sodom as Lot was sitting in the gate. He greeted them and offered them hospitality. They ate and spent the night.

In the morning the angels said to Lot, "This city will be destroyed because of its wickedness. Take your wife and your family and leave. Do not stop anywhere and do not look back."

But his wife, behind him, looked back,	וַתַּבֵּט אִשְׁתּוֹ מֵאַחֲרָיו
and she turned into a pillar of salt.	וַתְּהִי נְצִיב מֶלַח

36

The next morning Abraham looked down toward Sodom and Gomorrah, and he saw smoke rising like the smoke of a kiln. And so it was that when God destroyed the cities where Lot lived, He was considerate of Abraham and removed Lot from the midst of the destruction.

COMMENTARIES

From the Zohar

The people of Sodom and Gomorrah deserved to be punished. They were immoral and uncharitable. Whoever grudges assistance to the poor does not deserve to exist in the world, and he also gives up his place in the world-to-come. But whoever is generous to the poor deserves to exist in the world. The world exists for his sake, and he is assured a place in the world-to-come.

From the Midrash

The sin of the people of Sodom was not only in the evil things the people did. An even greater crime was that when they saw evil committed, they did not protest against it but allowed it to continue.

From the Talmud

The people of Sodom were very cruel to strangers. If a stranger came to their city, they would pretend to extend their hospitality and offer him a bed to sleep in for the night. All the beds were the same size. If the stranger was too big for the bed, they tried to force him into it until he was near death. But if the stranger was too short, they pulled and stretched him until he filled it. When the stranger cried out in pain, they would say, "This will be done to anyone who comes to visit our city."

FOCUS ON VALUES:

Sometimes we are influenced to do wrong things by those around us, things we would not do if friends or other people did not persuade us. Our ancient rabbis were aware of this danger. In discussing the destruction of Sodom and Gomorrah in the Mishnah, the rabbis advised that if a person could not find ten good people in a city, he should move away.

A QUESTION OF VALUES

Contrast the above Mishnah with the stories of Abraham's graciousness and hospitality. Do you think the story you just read has a point other than to show the wickedness of the Sodomites?

God did as He had promised. Sarah had a son, and Abraham named him Isaac. When Isaac was eight days old, Abraham circumcised him, as God had commanded him. Sarah said, "God has brought me laughter. Everyone who hears will laugh with me."

Ishmael was the son of Hagar the Egyptian and Abraham. When Sarah saw him playing, she said to Abraham, "Send away that slavewoman with her son, for the son of that slave shall not share in the inheritance with my son Isaac." Abraham was upset because it concerned a son of his. But God said, "Do as Sarah tells you, for it is through Isaac that your descendants will be continued for you. As for the son of the slavewoman, I will make a nation of him too, for he is your offspring."

The next day Abraham sent Hagar and Ishmael away, and they wandered in the wilderness of Beersheba. Hagar put the child under one of the bushes and sat at a distance. There was no water, and she did not want to watch the child die. But God called to Hagar,

"Come,	קוּמִי
lift up the boy	שְׂאִי אֶת־הַנַּעַר
and hold him by the hand,	וְהַחֲזִיקִי אֶת־יָדֵךְ בּוֹ
for I will make a great nation of him."	כִּי־לְגוֹי גָּדוֹל אֲשִׂימֶנּוּ.

Ishmael grew up and lived in the wilderness. His mother got a wife for him from the land of Egypt.

VI
God Tests Abraham

Genesis 22:1—23:20

God tests Abraham by asking him to offer Isaac as a sacrifice. Abraham prepares to offer his son up as a burnt offering, but at the last moment, God intercedes, and Abraham instead sacrifices a ram.

Later, Sarah dies, and Abraham buries her in the Cave of Machpelah, which he buys for four hundred shekels of silver.

Summary: GENESIS 22:1—8

God tested Abraham. He called to him and said, "Abraham," and Abraham answered, "Here I am." And God said, "Take your son whom you love to the land of Moriah, and offer him there as a burnt offering on one of the mountains I will show you."

Abraham set out the next morning with his son Isaac and two of his servants. On the third day, Abraham looked up and saw the place in the distance. Then Abraham said to his servants, "You stay here, and the boy and I will go up on the mountain. We will worship, and then we will return to you."

Abraham took the wood for the burnt offering and put it on his son, Isaac. He himself took the firestone and the knife, and the two walked off together.

Then Isaac said to his father, "Here is the firestone and the wood; but where is the sheep for the sacrifice?"

"God will see to the sheep for   אֱלֹהִים יִרְאֶה־לּוֹ הַשֶּׂה לְעֹלָה
    the burnt offering,
my son."   בְּנִי.

And the two of them walked on together.

COMMENTARIES

From Maimonides

The question arises, Why did God test Abraham? Since God knows all things, He must have known that Abraham would pass the test.

But that is exactly the reason why God did test Abraham in this way. He knew that Abraahm would not refuse to sacrifice Isaac, and so Abraham's willing response would serve as an example to people of future generations to obey God's commandments.

From the Midrash

The place where Abraham built the altar to sacrifice Isaac was the same spot where Adam brought his first sacrifice to God, and where Cain and Abel had brought their sacrifices. It was also the same spot where Noah built an altar after he came out of the ark.

On this spot would one day be built the Bet Hamikdash, the Holy Temple.

When Abraham and Isaac arrived at the place which God had told Abraham, Abraham built an altar. He placed wood on it. Then he tied his son Isaac and placed him on the altar on top of the wood.

Abraham picked up the knife to kill his son. But an angel of God called to him from heaven, "Abraham, Abraham, do not raise your hand against the boy or do anything to him. For now I know that you fear God, since you have not withheld even your son from Me."

When Abraham looked up, he saw a ram caught in the thicket by its horns. Abraham took the ram and offered it as a burnt offering in place of his son.

The angel of God called to Abraham a second time from heaven and said, "Because you have done this and have not withheld your son,

I will bestow My blessing on you	כִּי־בָרֵךְ אֲבָרֶכְךָ
and make your descendants as many as the stars of heaven	וְהַרְבָּה אַרְבֶּה אֶת־זַרְעֲךָ כְּכוֹכְבֵי הַשָּׁמַיִם
and the sands of the seashore,	וְכַחוֹל אֲשֶׁר עַל־שְׂפַת הַיָּם
and your descendants shall be victorious over their enemies,	וְיִרַשׁ זַרְעֲךָ אֵת שַׁעַר אֹיְבָיו:
and all the nations of the earth shall bless themselves by your descendants,	וְהִתְבָּרֲכוּ בְזַרְעֲךָ כֹּל גּוֹיֵי הָאָרֶץ
because you obeyed My command."	עֵקֶב אֲשֶׁר שָׁמַעְתָּ בְּקֹלִי:

Abraham then returned to his servants, and they left together for Beersheba, and Abraham stayed in Beersheba.

42

COMMENTARIES

From the Talmud

We blow the shofar made from a ram's horn on Rosh Hashana to remind God of Abraham's willingness to sacrifice his son Isaac. Perhaps when God remembers the righteousness of our ancestor, Abraham, He will forgive our own sins more leniently.

From the Midrash

After these events Abraham spoke to God and said, "When You first told me to sacrifice Isaac, I did not understand. Long ago You told me that I would be the father of a great nation through the descendants of Isaac. Then You told me to sacrifice this same son, Isaac. I could have argued with You, but I held back. Now I would like something from You. When the childen of Isaac in years to come sin against You, remember my willingness to obey Your command and sacrifice my son, Isaac, and for my sake, forgive the sins of the descendants of Isaac and treat them kindly." It was God Himself who ordered Abraham to sacrifice his son. But it was an angel who saved Isaac. From this we learn that only God Himself can order the death of a human being, but even the smallest angel can show mercy and save a life.

SOMETHING TO THINK ABOUT

Do you think it is ever justified for one human being to take the life of another? What about: In a war? In self-defense? As capital punishment?

Sarah died at the age of 127 years in Kiriath-Arba, now Hebron, in the land of Canaan. And Abraham mourned for her and cried. Then Abraham spoke to the children of Heth and said, "Sell me a burial site that I may remove my dead for burial."

Although he was offered a free burial spot for Sarah, Abraham insisted on paying for it. Finally he purchased the Cave of Machpelah for four hundred shekels of silver, which was the going merchants' rate.

Then Abraham buried his wife Sarah	וְאַחֲרֵי־כֵן קָבַר אַבְרָהָם אֶת־שָׂרָה אִשְׁתּוֹ
in the cave of the field of Machpelah	אֶל־מְעָרַת שְׂדֵה הַמַּכְפֵּלָה
facing Mamre, now Hebron,	עַל־פְּנֵי מַמְרֵא הִוא חֶבְרוֹן
in the land of Canaan.	בְּאֶרֶץ כְּנָעַן.

COMMENTARIES

From the Midrash

Sarah died because Isaac did not return with Abraham and she believed that he had been sacrificed. She died of a broken heart.

LEARNING MORE ABOUT PLACES IN THE BIBLE:
BEERSHEBA

The city of Beersheba is mentioned frequently in the early portions of the Bible. We are told that Abraham dug a well there and planted a tamarisk tree. Beersheba is the city to which Abraham and Isaac returned after Abraham almost sacrificed his son to God.

Beersheba is the northern gateway to the Negev. In Biblical times it was the rallying place for the tribes of Israel. When Rome ruled the area, Beersheba was a prosperous caravan station on the route from Eilat to the Mediterranean Sea. After the Arab invasion, it lay desolate for many centuries.

Today, Beersheba is a flourishing Israeli city. There are hotels, apartment houses, stores, and a well-known university. Many Israelis live there, and many Israelis and tourists come to visit this modern-ancient city that goes back to Bible times.

Thursday is market day in Beersheba. On Thursday the Bedouin farmers and herdsmen converge on the city to sell and trade their produce and animals.

VII

A Bride for Isaac

Genesis 24:1–25:18

Abraham sends his trusted servant (Eliezer) to the land of his birth to find a wife for his son Isaac.

(Eliezer) travels to the city where Abraham's brother, Nahor, lives and there meets the beautiful and kind Rebecca, Nahor's granddaughter. He brings her home to become the bride of Isaac.

After a number of years Abraham dies and is buried in the Cave of Machpelah with Sarah.

Summary: GENESIS 24:1–21

Abraham was old, and the Lord had blessed him in all things. And Abraham said to his senior servant, who was in charge of all that he owned, "Swear that you will not allow my son to marry a Canaanite, but go to the land of my birth and find a wife for my son, Isaac."

The servant said, "What if the woman does not agree to come to this land? Shall I bring your son back to the land from which you came?"

Abraham answered, "On no account may you take my son back there! If the woman does not agree to come back here, then you are free of your obligation."

The servant took ten of his master's camels and gifts from his master's treasures, and went to the city of Abraham's brother, Nahor. He stopped at the well outside the city at evening time, when women came to draw water. There he prayed to God.

"O Lord, God of my master Abraham, let the young woman to whom I speak and ask for a drink, and she replies that she will give me a drink and also draw water for my camels, be the one that you have chosen for Isaac."

He had scarcely finished speaking when Rebecca, the daughter of Bethuel and the granddaughter of Nahor, came to the well with the jar on her shoulder. She was very beautiful.

The servant ran to her and said, "Please let me sip a little water from your jar."

"Drink, sir," she said, and lowered her jar so that he might drink.

When he had finished drinking, she said,

"I will also draw water for your camels	גַּם לִגְמַלֶּיךָ אֶשְׁאָב
until they finish drinking."	עַד אִם־כִּלּוּ לִשְׁתֹּת.

And she ran back to the well to draw water for his camels.

COMMENTARIES

From the Midrash

Rebecca was not only beautiful, she was also very kind. Although she was rich and did not have to go to the well to draw water, since she had many servants who could have done it for her, she nevertheless went to the well every day so that she could meet the townspeople and help those who needed help.

Asking whether the camels also needed water was a sign that Rebecca had a kind heart. Kindness to animals is an important virtue in Judaism. The Talmud says that a person must not sit down to his own meal until all his animals have been fed.

When his camels had finished drinking, the servant took a gold nose ring and two gold bracelets and gave them to Rebecca.

"Whose daughter are you?" he asked, "And is there room in your father's house for us to spend the night?"

She answered, "I am the daughter of Bethuel, who is the son of Nahor, and there is plenty of room in my home for you to spend the night."

Eliezer knew that his prayer had been answered and that he had been guided to the house of his master's relatives. He bowed and thanked God.

Meanwhile, Rebecca ran home and told her family about what had happened to her. When her brother Laban heard the story and saw the nose ring and bracelets that Eliezer had given Rebecca, he ran out to meet him, invited him into the house, and offered him food. But Eliezer would not eat until he had told his story and asked for Rebecca to become the wife of Isaac.

Laban and Bethuel answered, "This has been arranged by God; we cannot express an opinion, good or bad. But let us call the girl and ask for her reply."

They called Rebecca and said to her,	וַיִּקְרְאוּ לְרִבְקָה וַיֹּאמְרוּ אֵלֶיהָ
"Will you go with this man?"	הֲתֵלְכִי עִם־הָאִישׁ הַזֶּה
And she said, "I will."	וַתֹּאמֶר אֵלֵךְ׃

COMMENTARIES

From the Midrash

Laban and Bethuel did not consent to Rebecca's marriage to Isaac. They asked her what *her* wishes were and whether she wanted to go with Eliezer and marry Isaac.

From this we learn that a woman cannot be given in marriage against her will. She must be asked, and she must give her consent.

Rebecca went with Abraham's servant and traveled to the land where Abraham and Isaac lived. As they approached, Isaac, who was out walking in the field, looked up and saw the camels approaching. Rebecca looked up and saw Isaac.

"Who is that man?" she asked.

"That is my master, Isaac," said the servant.

So she took her veil and covered herself. And Eliezer told Isaac all that had happened. Isaac then brought her into the tent of his mother, Sarah, and Rebecca became his wife.

Isaac loved her	וַיֶּאֱהָבֶהָ
and found comfort	וַיִּנָּחֵם יִצְחָק
after his mother's death.	אַחֲרֵי אִמּוֹ׃

COMMENTARIES

From the Midrash

For three years Isaac had mourned for his mother, Sarah. Nothing could console him. But when he married Rebecca, he was comforted for the death of his mother.

Not only did Rebecca occupy Sarah's tent, she was her successor in other ways as well. Sarah had been a very kind and charitable person. Rebecca continued to give freely to those in need, as had her mother-in-law. The door of her tent was always open to the poor and to all who needed help.

Abraham married again before he died and had other children. But he willed all that he owned to Isaac. To his other chidren he gave gifts while he was still living and sent them away to the Land of the East, away from his son Isaac.

Abraham lived 175 years and died at a good ripe old age. His sons Isaac and Ishmael buried him in the Cave of Machpelah. After the death of Abraham, God blessed his son Isaac. And Ishmael lived to be 137 years old and had children who became the chieftains of many tribes.

VIII
Jacob and Esau

Genesis 25:19–28:9

*Isaac and Rebecca become the parents of twin sons,
Jacob and Esau. Esau, the elder, is entitled to his
father's blessing, but he sells his birthright to Jacob for
a bowl of lentil stew.*

*When it is time for Isaac to bless his older son, Esau,
Rebecca and Jacob trick him into giving Jacob the
blessing.*

*Esau is very angry at Jacob, and Jacob must run away
to escape his brother's anger.*

Summary: GENESIS 25:19–34

Twin sons were born to Isaac and Rebecca. The first one was
named Esau, and the second was named Jacob. When the boys
grew up, Esau became a skillful hunter, a man of the outdoors;
but Jacob was a mild man who stayed in camp. Isaac preferred
Esau, because he liked to eat the meat of the animals that Esau
the hunter caught. But Rebecca loved Jacob.

Once, when Jacob was cooking a stew, Esau came in from
the field, and he was very hungry. He said to Jacob, "Give me
some of that red stuff to eat. I am very hungry."

But Jacob said, "I will if you will first sell me your birthright."

"What use is my birthright to me if I starve to death?" said
Esau, and he sold his birthright to his brother Jacob for a bowl of
lentil stew.

Jacob gave Esau bread and
lentil stew;
and he ate and drank
and went on his way.
Thus did Esau reject the birthright.

וְיַעֲקֹב נָתַן לְעֵשָׂו לֶחֶם וּנְזִיד
עֲדָשִׁים
וַיֹּאכַל וַיֵּשְׁתְּ
וַיָּקָם וַיֵּלַךְ
וַיִּבֶז עֵשָׂו אֶת־הַבְּכֹרָה.

COMMENTARIES

From Rashi

Jacob "stayed in camp" and did not engage in outdoor activities because he spent all his time in study and meditation so that he could learn all about God.

From the Midrash

Jacob deserved to have the birthright even though he was the younger of the two brothers, because Esau was wicked from the moment he was born.

Both Jacob and Esau tried to influence those around them. Jacob tried to turn them toward God, while Esau tried to turn them away from God.

SOMETHING TO THINK ABOUT

There are many people who try to influence us to behave in a particular way. Our parents and teachers try to influence us to become better people. Our friends and acquaintances also influence our behavior. Sometimes these are good influences and sometimes they are bad. How can we know the difference? What can we do to resist those who try to influence us wrongly?

When Isaac was old and his eyes were too dim to see, he called his older son, Esau, and said, "I am old and do not know how soon I will die. Take your bow and arrows, and go out into the country and hunt me some game. Then cook it for me as I like it, and bring it to me to eat. Then I will give you my blessing."

Rebecca overheard Isaac talking to Esau. She called Jacob and said to him, "Bring me two choice kids from the flock, and I will cook them as your father likes. Then take them to your father to eat, and he will bless you."

Jacob answered, "My brother is a hairy man, and my skin is smooth. If my father touches me, he will know that he has been tricked, and he will curse me instead of blessing me."

But Rebecca said, "Just do as I say."

Jacob brought all the things his mother had asked for, and she prepared a tasty dish such as his father liked. Then Rebecca took Esau's best clothes and had her younger son, Jacob, put them on, and she covered his hands and neck with the skins of animals and had him bring to his father the food that she had prepared.

When Jacob came to his father, his father asked, "Which of my sons are you?"

Jacob answered, "I am Esau, your firstborn."

"Come close to me," said Isaac, "so that I may feel you."

Jacob came close to his father, who said as he felt him,

"The voice is the voice of Jacob,	הַקֹּל קוֹל יַעֲקֹב
but the hands are the hands of Esau."	וְהַיָּדַיִם יְדֵי עֵשָׂו.

53

Isaac did not recognize Jacob because his hands were hairy, and his clothing, which was Esau's, smelled of the field. And Isaac blessed Jacob saying, "May God give you of the dew of heaven and the fat of the earth, and may you have an abundance of grain and wine. Let peoples serve you, and nations bow to you. Be master over your brothers, and let them bow to you. May those who bless you be blessed and those who curse you be cursed."

COMMENTARIES

From the Midrash

Jacob was never able to enjoy the heritage. He felt guilty all his life because he had deceived his brother and taken his blessing and his inheritance.

The "voice of Jacob" stands for Torah and truth. The "hands of Esau" stand for force and violence. As long as there is Torah and truth in the world, there can be no violence. As long as the Jew allows the "voice of Jacob" to be his guide, the "hands of Esau" cannot harm him.

No sooner had Isaac finished blessing Jacob than Esau returned from his hunt. He, too, prepared a tasty dish and brought it to his father. Then he asked for his father's blessing.

"Who are you?" asked Isaac.	וַיֹּאמֶר לוֹ יִצְחָק אָבִיו מִי־אָתָּה
"I am Esau, your firstborn," answered Esau.	וַיֹּאמֶר אֲנִי בִּנְךָ בְּכֹרְךָ עֵשָׂו׃

Isaac began to tremble. "Who was it to whom I gave my blessing?" he asked. "I blessed him, and now he must remain blessed."

When Esau heard his father's words he began to sob bitterly. "Bless me, too, father," he said. But Isaac answered, "I blessed him and made him master over you. You shall enjoy the fat of the earth and the dew of heaven above. But you shall live by your sword, and you shall serve your brother."

Now Esau held a grudge against his brother because of the blessing, and he swore to kill him. But Rebecca sent Jacob to live with her brother Laban until Esau's anger had subsided and he no longer carried a grudge for what Jacob had done to him.

COMMENTARIES

From the Midrash

At first Isaac felt great anguish because he had given the blessing to the younger son, Jacob. But when he was told that Esau had sold Jacob the birthright, he said, "I gave my blessing to the right one."
Although Jacob knew that Esau wanted to kill him, he was very courageous and would not run away. But Rebecca begged him to go so that his brother would not kill him and she would not have to mourn for both her sons.

55

SOMETHING TO THINK ABOUT

Was Jacob right to scheme to get the birthright from his brother? The ancient rabbis said that Jacob was justified because he was a better person than Esau and therefore would be a better leader for his people. Do you agree?

IX

Jacob's Dream

Genesis 28:10—36:43

Jacob leaves Beersheba and sets out for Haran. On the way, he stops to rest and dreams of angels, who tell him that the land he is on will one day belong to his descendants.

As Jacob approaches Haran, he meets his uncle Laban and Laban's daughter Rachel. He falls in love with Rachel and works seven years for her father so that she will become his bride. But Laban tricks him and substitutes Rachel's sister, Leah. Jacob works another seven years and marries Rachel.

Jacob prospers in Haran, but after a while he leaves with his family to return to his homeland. On his return home, he dreams again—this time of wrestling with an angel who changes his name to Israel.

Jacob and Esau are reunited, and Jacob settles down with his wives and sons. After a time Isaac dies, and his sons bury him.

Summary: GENESIS 28:10—22

Jacob left Beersheba and set out for Haran. He came upon a certain place and stopped there for the night. There he lay down with a stone for a pillow under his head. As he lay there, he dreamed that he saw a stairway with angels of God climbing up and down. And God stood beside him and said, "I am the God of your father Abraham and the God of Isaac.

The ground on which you are lying	הָאָרֶץ אֲשֶׁר אַתָּה שֹׁכֵב עָלֶיהָ
I will give to you	לְךָ אֶתְּנֶנָּה וּלְזַרְעֶךָ.
and to your descendants.	

57

Your descendants shall be as the dust of the earth, and you shall be spread out to the west, the east, the north, and the south. All the families of the earth shall bless themselves by you and your descendants. I am with you and will protect you wherever you go, and I will bring you back to this land."

When Jacob arose from his sleep he said, "Surely God is in this place," and he took the stone that had been under his head and made an altar to God and took a vow that the Lord would be his God forever.

COMMENTARIES

From the Midrash

When God promised to make Jacob's children as the dust of the earth, He meant that just as the earth survives all things, so too, shall Jacob's children survive all the nations of the earth. But just as the earth is stepped on, so will Jacob's children be stepped on and persecuted by the nations of the earth if they commit sins.

Jacob continued his journey and came to the land of the easterners. There he met some shepherds who were from Haran. Jacob asked, "Do you know Laban the son of Nahor?" and they said, "We do, and there is his daughter Rachel coming with the flock."

When Jacob saw Rachel, the daughter of Laban, his mother's brother, he kissed her and broke into tears. He told her that he was her father's relative—that he was Rebecca's son, and Rachel ran and told her father.

When Laban heard the news of his sister's son, he ran to greet Jacob and kissed him and took him into his house. Jacob worked for Laban for one month without wages. Laban offered to pay him for his service, but Jacob asked only that he be allowed to marry Laban's beautiful daughter, Rachel.

Jacob served Laban for seven years so that he could marry Rachel. Because he loved her, the time seemed to him as just a few days. Laban gathered all the people together for a wedding feast. But when evening came, he tricked Jacob and instead of marrying him to Rachel, he married Jacob to Rachel's older sister, Leah.

In the morning Jacob discovered that his bride was Leah instead of Rachel. "What have you done to me?" he asked Laban. "I worked for seven years for Rachel, and you tricked me and substituted Leah. Why did you deceive me?"

Laban said, "It is our custom to marry off the older before the younger. But if you will work for me another seven years, you may also marry Rachel."

So Jacob served Laban for seven more years, and Rachel, too, became his wife.

Jacob and his wives stayed on in Laban's house for another seven years after that. Jacob continued to serve Laban as before, and Laban prospered as a result of Jacob's service. During the time that Jacob lived in Laban's house he became the father of eleven sons, Reuben, Simeon, Levi, Judah, Dan, Naphtali, Gad, Asher, Issachar, Zebulun, and Joseph. But only Joseph was the son of his favored wife, Rachel.

The time came when Jacob saw that Laban's behavior toward him was not as it had been in the past. Then God said to Jacob,

"Return to the land of your fathers, to your birth-place and I will be with you." שׁוּב אֶל־אֶרֶץ אֲבוֹתֶיךָ וּלְמוֹלַדְתֶּךָ וְאֶהְיֶה עִמָּךְ:

So Jacob put his wives and children on camels, and he took with him all his livestock and the wealth that he had accumulated to go to his father, Isaac, in the land of Canaan. Soon he was across the Euphrates and heading toward the hill country of Gilead. But Laban pursued Jacob and caught up to him in Gilead, where they made a covenant and parted in peace. And Jacob continued on his journey.

COMMENTARIES

From the Midrash

Jacob did not discover that he had been tricked by Laban and given the wrong wife until the morning after the wedding, because every time he spoke to Leah in the dark and called her Rachel, she answered him as if she really were Rachel. When morning came and he could see that Leah had been substituted for Rachel, he was angry and scolded Leah for deceiving him.

"I have been a good student," said Leah. "I learned from you how to deceive. When your father called you Esau before he bestowed the blessing, didn't you answer, 'Here I am.'"

The townspeople who were Laban's guests at the wedding of Jacob and Leah helped Laban carry out the deception. Before Jacob came to live with Laban, there had been a scarcity of water in the area. But because of Jacob's goodness, God blessed the entire area so that there was plenty of water.

When Laban was getting ready for the wedding, he called all the townspeople together and said to them,

"I have a plan that will keep Jacob in my house for an additional seven years, and we will all have plenty of water during that time." And Laban told them of the trick he was planning.

The townspeople agreed to go along with Laban and not betray him to Jacob.

Summary: GENESIS 32:1–34:31

Jacob sent messengers ahead to his brother Esau, in the land of
Seir, the country of Edom, and instructed them to say that Jacob
had returned with great wealth and was seeking to make peace
with his brother.

The messengers returned with the report that Esau was on his
way to meet Jacob with four hundred men. Jacob was frightened
and prayed to God. Then he selected lavish gifts for Esau and sent
them ahead. He and his family spent the night in camp while they
awaited Esau's response.

That night, when Jacob was alone, a man wrestled with him
until the break of dawn. Jacob grabbed the man and would not let
go until the other blessed him. And the man said, "What is your
name?" and Jacob answered, "It is Jacob." And the man said,
"You will no longer be called Jacob, but you will be 'Israel,' for
you have struggled with a divine being and you have won."

And Jacob named the place Peniel, which means, "I have
seen a divine being face to face and my life has been preserved."

Then Jacob looked up and saw his brother Esau, followed by
four hundred men. Jacob went ahead and bowed low to the
ground seven times before his brother, and Esau ran to greet him,
and they embraced and kissed and cried. And Jacob said,

"Please accept my gift;	וְלָקַחְתָּ מִנְחָתִי מִיָּדִי
for to see your face	כִּי עַל־כֵּן רָאִיתִי פָנֶיךָ
is like seeing the face of God,	כִּרְאֹת פְּנֵי אֱלֹהִים
and you have received me favorably."	וַתִּרְצֵנִי:

Esau started back that day to Seir, and Jacob journeyed to
Succoth, where he built a house for himself and stalls for his cattle.

61

COMMENTARIES

From the Midrash

As Jacob prepared to meet Esau, he was very concerned that Esau might now be God's favorite instead of himself. Jacob knew that for the past twenty years Esau had been fulfilling two important commandments that he had unavoidably ignored. Esau had been living in the Holy Land, while Jacob had lived outside it; and Esau had taken care of his elderly parents, Isaac and Rebecca, while Jacob could not because he lived such a distance from them.

From Rashi

As Jacob approached Esau he was very fearful. Not only was he afraid that Esau might harm him, but he was afraid that Esau might attack him and he would be forced to fight back and harm Esau.

SOMETHING TO THINK ABOUT

Golda Meir, the late Prime Minister of Israel, once expressed a feeling similar to the one described by Rashi when she said that the Israelis could forgive their enemies for killing Israeli boys, but the Israelis could not forgive their enemies for making it necessary for Israeli boys to kill enemy soldiers.

What do you think that both Rashi and Golda Meir were trying to say?

Jacob continued on his journey and came to Bethel in the land of Canaan. There he built an altar and named the place El-Bethel, for it was there that God had revealed Himself to him when he was fleeing from his brother.

When Jacob arrived from Paddan-Aram, God again appeared to him and blessed him.

God said to him,	וַיֹּאמֶר־לוֹ אֱלֹהִים
"You, whose name is Jacob,	שִׁמְךָ יַעֲקֹב
shall be called Jacob no more.	לֹא־יִקָּרֵא שִׁמְךָ עוֹד יַעֲקֹב
But Israel shall be your name."	כִּי אִם־יִשְׂרָאֵל יִהְיֶה שְׁמֶךָ.

Then God said, "I am El Shaddai. Be fertile and increase. A nation shall descend from you, and you shall be the ancestor of kings. The land that I gave to Abraham and Isaac, I give to you; and to your offspring to come will I give the land."

Jacob built an altar and offered a sacrifice. Then he and those with him set out once more to continue their journey. Before they had reached their destination, Rachel gave birth to another child, and Jacob called him Benjamin. But Rachel died in childbirth, and Jacob buried her on the road to Ephrath, which is now Bethlehem.

When Jacob was reunited with his father, Isaac, at Mamre, at Kiriath-Arba, which is now Hebron, Isaac was 180 years old. When he breathed his last and died, he was buried by his sons Esau and Jacob.

COMMENTARIES

From the Midrash

When Jacob arrived at his destination, he immediately bought a parcel of land, for it is the duty of every person who can afford it to buy land in the Holy Land when he comes there from the outside.

LEARNING MORE ABOUT BIBLICAL COMMENTARIES: RASHI

Many of the Biblical commentaries in this book are from Rabbi Solomon Yitzhaki, who is almost always referred to by the Hebrew abbreviation of his name, Rashi.

Rashi is one of the best-known of all the commentators on the Bible, and he is often quoted by rabbis and scholars. He was not only a Biblical and Talmudic commentator but a beloved figure in Jewish history. There are many legends about his goodness and his deeds.

Rashi lived in the eleventh century. He was born in Troyes, France, and spent a short time studying in Worms, Germany. He founded a school for the study of Talmud in France. This school soon became very famous and attracted students from all over the world. Sometimes Rashi's students had difficulty understanding the Talmud. Rashi believed that this was so because there wasn't a really good commentary on the Talmud. So Rashi wrote one. Soon his commentary was a standard guide for every student who studied the Talmud.

Rashi's commentaries are printed in a unique Hebrew script, very unlike the usual Hebrew printing. Before a student can even start studying the commentaries, he or she must first learn to read "Rashi script." But most students think that it is worth the effort because of the importance of the commentary and the wealth of material it contains.

Rashi script.

מלךכיטחוהדגבצק

חשרקזלתפעסנוס

X

Joseph and His Brothers

Genesis 37:1−36

Joseph, the favorite son of Jacob, dreams that he will one day rule over his brothers. His jealous brothers plot against him, finally throwing him into a pit, from which he is taken by traders and sold as a slave in Egypt.

The brothers, ashamed and frightened because of what they have done, dip Joseph's clothes in the blood of an animal and tell Jacob that Joseph has been killed by wild animals.

Summary: GENESIS 37:1−10

Jacob settled with his family in the land where his father had lived, the land of Canaan. There, Joseph tended the flocks as a helper to his brothers, and Joseph brought bad reports about his brothers to his father.

Jacob loved Joseph best of all his sons, for he was the son of his old age, and Jacob made a multicolored coat for Joseph. When Joseph's brothers saw that Jacob loved Joseph more than any of his brothers, they hated him and could not speak a friendly word to him.

One day, Joseph had a dream which he told to his brothers, and they hated him even more. He said to them, "Listen to my dream. In it, we were all tying sheaves of wheat in the field, when suddenly my sheaf stood up and remained standing upright. Then your sheaves all gathered around and bowed down to my sheaf."

His brothers answered, וַיֹּאמְרוּ לוֹ אֶחָיו

"Do you mean that you will הֲמָלֹךְ תִּמְלֹךְ עָלֵינוּ אִם־מָשׁוֹל
be our king and rule over תִּמְשֹׁל בָּנוּ
us?"

And they hated him even וַיּוֹסִפוּ עוֹד שְׂנֹא אֹתוֹ.
more."

Then Joseph dreamed another dream and told it to his brothers. This time the sun, the moon, and eleven stars all bowed down to him. When he told this dream to his father and brothers, his father scolded him. "What is this dream you dreamed?" he said. "Will your mother and I and all your brothers bow down to you?"

COMMENTARIES

From the Midrash

It was part of God's plan to get Joseph into Egypt in order that he might in future years be able to save his family. The preference Jacob showed for his son Joseph and the jealousy of the brothers were just disguised means for getting Joseph into Egypt.

From Nachmanides

When Joseph related his second dream, that is, that the sun, moon, and eleven stars would bow to him, Jacob scolded Joseph, not because he himself was angry, but because he knew of the anger of Joseph's brothers and wanted to dissipate some of that anger.

66

One time, when Joseph's brothers were tending their sheep at
Shechem, Jacob sent Joseph to see how his brothers and the sheep
were and to bring back word. When Joseph approached, the
brothers saw him in the distance, and they conspired to kill him.

They said to one another, "Here comes the dreamer. Come,
let us kill him and throw him into one of the pits. Then we can say
that a wild beast ate him. We will see what comes of his dreams."

But when Reuben heard, he tried to save him from them. He
said, "Let us not take his life and not shed blood. Cast him into
that pit in the wilderness, but do not touch him yourselves."
Reuben intended to save Joseph and bring him back to his father.

When Joseph reached his brothers, they stripped him of his
multicolored coat and took him and cast him into the pit. Then
they sat down to eat.

When they looked up they saw a caravan of Ishmaelites
carrying goods to Egypt. Then Judah said to his brothers,

"What do we gain by killing our brother	מַה־בֶּצַע כִּי נַהֲרֹג אֶת־אָחִינוּ
and covering up his blood?	וְכִסִּינוּ אֶת־דָּמוֹ:
Let us sell him to the Ishmaelites."	לְכוּ וְנִמְכְּרֶנּוּ לַיִּשְׁמְעֵאלִים
After all, he is our brother, our own flesh."	כִּי־אָחִינוּ בְשָׂרֵנוּ הוּא

The brothers agreed. They pulled Joseph out of the pit and
sold him for twenty pieces of silver to the traders, who brought
Joseph to Egypt.

COMMENTARIES

From Nachmanides

Reuben would not let his brothers kill Joseph by shedding his blood and suggested instead that they place him in a cave, where he would die from lack of air and starvation. He reasoned that the punishment for actually taking a life was more severe than that for standing by and allowing another to die. But Judah said, "Allowing him to die in the cave will be accounted as a murder just as if we had killed him with our own hands."

Summary: GENESIS 37:29–36

When Reuben returned to the pit and saw that Joseph was not there, he tore his clothes. He returned to his brothers and said, "Joseph is gone. What am I to do?"

The brothers took Joseph's coat, killed a kid, and dipped the coat in the blood. They took it home to their father and said, "We found this. Please look at it. Is it your son's coat?"

Jacob recognized the coat. He believed that Joseph had been killed by a wild beast.

Jacob tore his clothes	וַיִּקְרַע יַעֲקֹב שִׂמְלֹתָיו
and put on sackcloth	וַיָּשֶׂם שַׂק בְּמָתְנָיו
and mourned for his son for many days.	וַיִּתְאַבֵּל עַל־בְּנוֹ יָמִים רַבִּים:

All Jacob's sons and daughters tried to comfort him, but he would not be comforted.

The traders, meanwhile, sold Joseph in Egypt to Potiphar, a courtier of Pharaoh and Pharaoh's chief steward.

COMMENTARIES

From the Midrash

When Reuben threw Joseph into the pit, he meant to return later and rescue him, but his brothers got to Joseph first, removed him from the pit, and sold him. Although Reuben's intentions were frustrated, he was well regarded by God, for God rewards not only good deeds but good intentions.

LEARNING MORE ABOUT:
ARCHAEOLOGY AND THE BIBLE

Archaeology is the study of ancient civilizations. Archaeologists study artifacts, objects used by people long ago, to reconstruct how ancient people lived and to get information about their history. Archaeologists find these artifacts by digging in the ruins of ancient civilizations.

One of the most fascinating fields of archaeological study is that of Biblical archaeology. The Biblical archaeologist tries to find relics of civilizations that existed in Bible times, and from them to reconstruct the history of the Biblical period. Often information from the Bible itself is used as a guide indicating where to dig for relics. Many of the places described in the Bible have been found by archaeologists digging in Israel.

Archaeologists are scientists. They are not trying to prove or disprove the Bible. But most archaeologists have found that the parts of the Bible that deal with history are quite accurate and can often be supported by other documents or by archaeological findings. Although the historical accuracy of many things in the Bible has not been tested and proved, no archaeological finding has as yet proved that any historical information in the Bible is untrue.

XI
Joseph in Egypt
Genesis 39:1–45:15

Joseph arrives safely in Egypt and through a series of fortunate events rises to high position there. His brothers come to Egypt seeking relief from a famine in Canaan and are at Joseph's mercy. But Joseph forgives his brothers and helps them. In a dramatic confrontation he reveals his identity and sends for his father, Jacob.

Summary: GENESIS 39:1–23

When Joseph was taken down to Egypt, a certain Egyptian, Potiphar, an officer of Pharaoh and Pharaoh's chief steward, bought him. The Lord was with Joseph, and he became successful and remained in Potiphar's house. Potiphar took a liking to Joseph and made him his personal attendant and put him in charge of his household.

Joseph was well built and handsome, and Potiphar's wife was infatuated with him and wanted Joseph to love her. But Joseph would not be disloyal to his master. Potiphar's wife was angry and falsely accused Joseph to her husband. He was furious and had Joseph put in prison.

The Lord was with Joseph	וַיְהִי יְהֹוָה אֶת־יוֹסֵף
and extended kindness to him	וַיֵּט אֵלָיו חָסֶד
and caused the chief jailer to act kindly to him.	וַיִּתֵּן חִנּוֹ בְּעֵינֵי שַׂר בֵּית־הַסֹּהַר.

The chief jailer put Joseph in charge of all the prisoners, and he did not supervise anything that was in Joseph's charge, because the Lord was with Joseph, and whatever he did the Lord made successful.

71

COMMENTARIES

From the Midrash

When Joseph was first sold to Potiphar and put in charge of his household, he was very happy. Things were particularly pleasant for him because he was at last removed from the jealousy and envy of his brothers. At home, his brothers had gotten angry whenever their father showed special favoritism to Joseph. But in Potiphar's household he could enjoy being his master's favorite without arousing anger or jealousy in anyone else.

When Potiphar's wife tried to tempt Joseph he considered giving in. But then he thought of his father, Jacob. "What will my father say?" he wondered, and he did what was right.

When Joseph was sent to prison by Potiphar, he remained there for ten years. The reason God allowed him to stay in prison for that long was to punish him for boasting to his brothers and acting as if he were better than they.

One day, while Joseph was in prison, the cupbearer and the baker of the king of Egypt displeased their master and were sent to prison. The chief jailer assigned Joseph to them, and he attended them.

After they had been in custody for some time, they both had dreams which caused them to be very upset. In the morning Joseph saw that they were depressed and asked, "Why do you appear so downcast today?"

"It is because we had dreams and there is no one here to explain them," they answered.

Joseph said, "Do not interpretations come from God? Tell me about it."

Then the chief cupbearer told Joseph his dream. He had dreamed about a vine with three branches. On the branches were grapes. He had squeezed the grapes into Pharaoh's cup and placed the cup in Pharaoh's hand.

Joseph said, "The three branches are three days. In three days you shall be restored to your post. When all is well with you again, please mention me to Pharaoh so that he will free me from this place."

Then Joseph interpreted the dream of the baker. The baker had dreamed of three baskets. Each one contained food prepared by the baker. Birds were eating the food from the baskets.

To the baker Joseph said, "The three baskets are three days. In three days Pharaoh shall have you put to death."

All happened as Joseph had said. But the cupbearer did not remember Joseph, and Joseph remained in prison.

COMMENTARIES

From the Midrash

When Joseph interpreted the dream of the baker, he told him only the meaning that applied to the baker personally. But Joseph knew that the dream had a much deeper meaning. The three baskets of the dream also stood for the three nations that would in future years conquer Israel: Babylonia, Greece, and Rome. In the end, God would eliminate the enemies of Israel, just as the birds ate the food from the three baskets.

Two more years passed. Then Pharaoh had a dream. He dreamed that seven handsome and sturdy cows grazed in the grass. As they grazed, seven lean, ugly cows came along and ate them up. Pharaoh fell asleep and dreamed a second time. This time he dreamed that seven healthy, solid ears of grain were swallowed up by seven thin ears of grain.

Pharaoh sent for all the magicians and wise men of Egypt, but no one could interpret his dream. Then the cupbearer remembered Joseph and told Pharaoh how Joseph had interpreted his dream correctly in prison. Pharaoh sent for Joseph and told him of the dreams. Joseph said, "Not I will interpret your dreams, but God will see to your welfare." Then Joseph told Pharaoh what the dreams meant.

"Pharaoh's dreams are the same," he said. "God has told Pharaoh what He is about to do. The seven healthy cows and the seven solid ears of grain are seven years. There will be seven years of plenty in the land. The seven lean and ugly cows and the seven thin ears of grain are seven years of famine that will follow the years of plenty. Let Pharaoh find a wise man and set him over the land of Egypt. Then let Pharaoh take steps to organize the land of Egypt during the seven years of plenty so that grain can be stored for the seven years of famine that will follow, and then the land will not perish."

The plan pleased Pharaoh and his courtiers. And Pharaoh put Joseph in charge of his court to organize the land and store grain for the seven years of famine. When Joseph was thirty years old, he was in charge of all of Egypt.

When the seven years of famine began just as Joseph had foretold, there was famine in all the lands. But throughout the land of Egypt there was bread, for grain had been stored during the years of plenty.

When all the land of Egypt felt the hunger,	וַתִּרְעַב כָּל־אֶרֶץ מִצְרַיִם
the people cried out to Pharaoh for bread.	וַיִּצְעַק הָעָם אֶל־פַּרְעֹה לַלָּחֶם
And Pharaoh said to all the Egyptians,	וַיֹּאמֶר פַּרְעֹה לְכָל־מִצְרַיִם
"Go to Joseph. Whatever he tells you, you will do."	לְכוּ אֶל־יוֹסֵף אֲשֶׁר־יֹאמַר לָכֶם תַּעֲשׂוּ.

The famine spread over the whole world, and all the world came to Joseph in Egypt to buy grain.

COMMENTARIES

From the Midrash

When there was no food left in Egypt, and the Egyptians were forced to go to Joseph for food, he said to them, "Give up your idol worship and bless God, who provides bread, and then I will give you food." But the Egyptians refused to give up their idol worship and complained to Pharaoh. Pharaoh said, "Do whatever Joseph says to you." For this, Pharaoh was rewarded with a long life and a long reign.

SOMETHING TO THINK ABOUT

According to the Midrash, Joseph used his powerful position in Egypt to make the Egyptians accept his beliefs. Do you think he was right in doing so? Would your opinion be the same if Joseph's beliefs did not agree with your own? Can you think of modern-day examples of powerful leaders using their positions of power to perpetuate their own beliefs and philosophies?

From Nachmanides

When food became less plentiful than it had been, the people came to Joseph begging for food. But he did not give away any food from the storehouses until there was no food at all left in the land. In this way he was able to preserve enough grain to last for the seven years when no food grew anywhere on earth.

SOMETHING TO THINK ABOUT

Does Joseph's decision, described in the Midrash, to deny food to the hungry Egyptians seem overly harsh? What would have happened if he had distributed all the food when the Egyptians first began to ask for it (that is, when they first began to feel the pangs of hunger)? How would you have handled this if you were in Joseph's position?

When Jacob heard that there was food to be had in Egypt, he sent ten of his sons there to buy food. But he did not send Benjamin, because he feared that something would happen to him.

Joseph's brothers came to Egypt and bowed low to the vizier of the land, Joseph. Though Joseph recognized his brothers, they did not recognize him, and he acted like a stranger to them and spoke harshly to them. And Joseph remembered the dreams he had dreamed about them when he was young.

Joseph said to his brothers, "You are spies and have come to see the land in its desolation." But his brothers said, "No, we have come to get food. We are all sons of the same man, honest men, who have never been spies. We were twelve brothers, sons of a certain man in Canaan. Our youngest brother is now with our father, and one is no more."

But Joseph said, "You are spies. You will be put to the test. Unless your youngest brother comes here, you will not be permitted to leave. Let one of you go and bring your brother, while the rest of you remain so that I can test if you are telling the truth." And Joseph put them in prison for three days.

On the third day, Joseph again said, "You must bring me your brother so that your words will be verified, or else you will all die."

They said to one another,	וַיֹּאמְרוּ אִישׁ אֶל־אָחִיו
"Alas, we are being punished	אֲבָל אֲשֵׁמִים אֲנַחְנוּ
on account of our brother,	עַל־אָחִינוּ
because we saw his pain,	אֲשֶׁר רָאִינוּ צָרַת נַפְשׁוֹ
but paid no attention while he	בְּהִתְחַנְנוֹ אֵלֵינוּ
pleaded with us."	וְלֹא שָׁמָעְנוּ.

78

Then Reuben said, "Didn't I tell you to do no wrong to the boy? But you did not listen. Now we are being punished."

They did not know that Joseph understood them. Joseph turned away and cried. But he continued to talk in the same manner. Then he took Simeon and had him bound before their eyes. He had the bags of the other brothers filled with grain, gave them provisions for their journey, and sent them on their way.

When they returned to their father, they told him all that had happened and that the vizier had ordered them to return with Benjamin.

But Jacob said, "My son must not go with you, for his brother is dead, and he alone is left. If he meets with disaster I will die."

COMMENTARIES

From the Midrash

Joseph's brothers, now older and wiser, regretted the way they had treated Joseph when they sold him to the Ishmaelite caravan. They knew that he must be somewhere in Egypt, and so when they went there to look for food during the famine, they planned to search for him and buy him back from his master. So anxious were they to find Joseph that, as they traveled, Joseph was even more in their thoughts than the original purpose of their trip, to buy food. They resolved that if their brother's master would not sell him back to them, they would use force to gain his release, even if they had to fight to the death.

SOMETHING TO THINK ABOUT

Joseph's brothers felt so guilty about having sold Joseph that they were willing to die fighting for his release. How had their attitudes changed in the years following their sale of Joseph? What do you think might have accounted for such a drastic change? Have you ever done something about which you felt guilty and wanted to make amends? Were you able to?

The famine in the land was very severe. When all the grain which Joseph's brothers had brought from Egypt was gone, Jacob asked his sons once more to go to Egypt and bring back more grain. But they were afraid of Joseph and would not go without their brother, Benjamin. Judah pledged that he would be responsible for Benjamin and guarantee his safety, and Jacob reluctantly allowed Benjamin to accompany his brothers to Egypt. The brothers took gifts for the vizier of Egypt, who was Joseph, and they traveled together to Egypt.

When Joseph saw that Benjamin had come with his brothers, he had his servants prepare a meal and invited the brothers to his home. They bowed low before Joseph and presented him with the gifts they had brought. Joseph greeted them and asked,

"How is your father of whom you spoke?" They replied, "It is well with our father. He is still in good health." And they again bowed down to Joseph.

After the brothers had enjoyed Joseph's hospitality and eaten at his table, Joseph instructed his servant to hide a silver goblet in the bag of the youngest brother, Benjamin. In the morning the brothers left the city. They had not gone far when Joseph sent his steward after them and instructed him to search for the silver goblet. "Tell them," he said, "that if the goblet is found in the bag of one of the brothers, that brother shall stay in Egypt and be my slave."

When the brothers saw that the goblet was in Benjamin's bag, they pleaded with Joseph not to keep Benjamin. Judah, who had pledged to his father that he would guarantee Benjamin's safety, offered to remain in Egypt and be Joseph's slave if only Benjamin would be allowed to return to his father.

COMMENTARIES

From the Midrash

Jacob was very reluctant to allow Benjamin to accompany his brothers to Egypt. He knew that there was a possibility that Benjamin would be enslaved in Egypt or even that he might die on the way. But he knew that if he did not allow Benjamin to go, there was a very good chance that he, his children, and his grandchildren would all die of starvation. Jacob weighed the risks against each other and decided to allow Benjamin to go.

Joseph could control himself no longer. He ordered everyone to leave his presence. Then he cried out to his brothers, "I am Joseph. Is my father still well?" But his brothers could not answer him, so dumbfounded were they.

Then Joseph said,   וַיֹּאמֶר

"I am your brother Joseph   אֲנִי יוֹסֵף אֲחִיכֶם

whom you sold into Egypt.   אֲשֶׁר־מְכַרְתֶּם אֹתִי מִצְרָיְמָה:

Do not reproach yourselves for what you did to me. It was to save life that God sent me ahead of you. I was sent to ensure your survival on earth and to save your lives. So it was not you who sent me here but God. Hurry back to my father and ask him to come to Egypt without delay, and he will live in the land of Goshen, where he will be near me. I will provide for him and his household for the remaining five years of famine. Tell my father everything about my high position in Egypt and all that you have seen, and bring my father here with all speed."

Then Joseph embraced Benjamin and wept. And Benjamin wept too. Joseph kissed all his brothers and wept. Only then were his brothers able to talk to him.

COMMENTARIES

From the Midrash

When Joseph extended an invitation to his father, Jacob, and to his brothers and their families to live in Egypt, some of his servants were fearful. They said, "Only one of Jacob's sons, Joseph, came to settle here, and he achieved such a high position and rules over us. If Jacob and his remaining sons come, they will one day take over our land and all rule over us."

Joseph's brothers returned to Canaan and reported to Jacob that Joseph was well and had achieved great wealth and power. But Jacob was not impressed. "Is he also charitable, kind, and God-fearing?" he asked. When he was assured that Joseph was all of those things, he raised his voice in prayer and thanked God for having preserved the life of his son Joseph.

From Rashi

Before Joseph made himself known to his brothers, he dismissed all his servants and courtiers from his presence. He did not want the Egyptians to witness the shame and embarrassment of his brothers when he made himself known to them.

From Nachmanides

Joseph dismissed the Egyptians from his presence before he made himself known to his brothers because he did not want them to hear the details of his sale to the caravan by his brothers. He did not want the Egyptians to say, "These are treacherous people who must not live in our land nor set foot in our palaces. They have dealt treacherously with their brother Joseph and their father. What will they do to the king and his people?"

XII

Jacob Comes to Egypt

Genesis 45:16–50:26

*Joseph sends for his father, Jacob, and the two are
reunited with tears and joy. Pharaoh welcomes Jacob
and his family, and they settle in Egypt, where they
prosper and increase greatly in numbers. But when
Jacob dies his sons carry him back to Canaan, the land
of his ancestors, and bury him in the Cave of Machpelah, which Abraham had bought for a burial site.*

*When Joseph is 110 years old, he too dies and is placed
in a coffin in Egypt, but not until he has exacted a
promise from his sons that when they leave Egypt they
will take his body back to Canaan.*

Summary: GENESIS 45:16–47:27

Joseph gave gifts to all his brothers. But to his brother Benjamin
he gave the most. He also sent gifts for his father, Jacob, and then
he sent his brothers on their way, urging them not to quarrel
among themselves.

When Jacob heard that Joseph was still alive, he offered
sacrifices to God at Beersheba and then set out with his sons, his
sons' wives, and his grandchildren to go to Egypt. They took their
livestock and the wealth they had amassed in Canaan and
brought it all with them to the land of Egypt.

The number of people who came with Jacob to Egypt, not
including the wives of his sons, was sixty-six. There were also two
of Joseph's sons who had been born in Egypt.

Thus the total of Jacob's household	הַנֶּפֶשׁ לְבֵית־יַעֲקֹב
who came to Egypt	הַבָּאָה מִצְרַיְמָה
was seventy persons.	שִׁבְעִים:

COMMENTARIES

From the Midrash

When Jacob's sons came back from Egypt and told their father that their brother Joseph was still alive, at first he did not believe them. Years before they had lied when they told their father that Joseph was dead. That time he did believe them. Now, when they told the truth, he did not believe them. So it is that liars are punished. Even when they tell the truth they are not believed.

Sixty-six members of Jacob's household left Canaan to go to Egypt. Joseph and his two sons add up to sixty-nine members of Jacob's household who came to Egypt. But the text says there were seventy members of Jacob's household in Egypt. The seventieth was God, who accompanied them to Egypt.

Jacob lived seventeen years in the land of Egypt. When the time approached for him to die, he called his son Joseph to him and asked him to swear that he would be buried in Canaan in the burial place of his ancestors. And Joseph swore.

Sometime afterward Joseph was told that his father was ill. He came to his father's bedside with his sons Manasseh and Ephraim. Jacob blessed Manasseh and Ephraim, and he blessed Joseph.

Then Jacob said to Joseph, "I am about to die; but God will be with you and will bring you back to the land of your ancestors."

After that Jacob called his sons	וַיִּקְרָא יַעֲקֹב אֶל־בָּנָיו
and said,	וַיֹּאמֶר
"Come together	הֵאָסְפוּ
that I may tell you	וְאַגִּידָה לָכֶם
what is to befall you	אֵת אֲשֶׁר־יִקְרָא אֶתְכֶם
in days to come."	בְּאַחֲרִית הַיָּמִים:

And Jacob blessed his sons and spoke of great things to come.

COMMENTARIES

From the Midrash

When Joseph heard that his father was ill, he went to visit him and brought with him his two sons, Ephraim and Manasseh. From this we learn that it is an obligation to visit the sick.

From the Talmud

All that Jacob said to his sons when he was dying was legally binding on them. The words of one who is dying are as binding as a written document.

86

Then Jacob again instructed his sons to bury him with his ancestors in the Cave of Machpelah in the land of Canaan. And Jacob died and was gathered to his people.

Joseph flung himself on his father's face and wept over him and kissed him. Then Joseph ordered the physicians in his service to embalm his father. And the Egyptians mourned him for seventy days. After that Joseph buried his father in the Cave of Machpelah, which Abraham had bought for a burial site. When he had buried his father, Joseph and all his brothers who had gone with him returned to Egypt.

Joseph remained in Egypt, and he lived for 110 years. He lived to see children of the third generation of Ephraim and Manasseh. When Joseph died he was embalmed and placed in a coffin in Egypt.

COMMENTARIES

From the Talmud

When Jacob died Joseph's brothers were afraid, now that their father was dead, that Joseph would turn against them and kill them. To protect themselves they lied to Joseph and told him that before he died Jacob had left instructions for Joseph to forgive his brothers and not harm them.

The rabbis said that the brothers could not be condemned for telling this lie. It is permissible to tell a white lie for the sake of peace.

SOMETHING TO THINK ABOUT

Have you ever told a "white lie"? Do you think it is ever right to lie? For example: Would you lie to spare a friend's feelings? Would you lie to save a person from harm? Would you lie to protect yourself?

From the Midrash

Joseph was a man of great kindness and compassion. In that way he showed that he was a true descendant of Abraham, Isaac, and Jacob. One who is merciful to his fellow man proves that he is a descendant of the Patriarchs, while one who is cruel to his fellow man proves that he cannot be a descendant of Abraham, Isaac, and Jacob.

LEARNING MORE ABOUT PLACES IN THE BIBLE: HEBRON

Hebron, also called Kiriath-Arba in the Bible, is the location of the Cave of Machpelah, the burial place of the patriarchs. The cave was bought by Abraham after Sarah's death so that he would have a burial site for her. It was bought from Ephron the Hittite for four hundred shekels of silver. Abraham, Isaac, Rebecca, and Jacob were later also buried there.

The Cave of Machpelah is an important religious shrine for Moslems as well as for Jews, since the Moslems also revere the patriarchs. Hebron was an Arab village for hundreds of years. During that time a mosque was built over what was believed to be the Cave of Machpelah.

Today, Hebron is a rapidly developing city. Much of the population is still Arab. But there is also a rapidly growing Jewish population, which lives in modern apartment houses. New industries have been developed, and a variety of products are manufactured there.

LEARNING MORE ABOUT PLACES IN THE BIBLE: EGYPT

Egypt is an ancient country whose recorded history goes back about six thousand years. From the very beginning it has been linked with the Jews and Jewish history. The patriarchs Abraham and Jacob visited Egypt; Joseph was the vizier of Egypt; and Jewish history begins with the Exodus from slavery in Egypt.

Egyptian and Jewish history have been intertwined through the ages. King Solomon was married to an Egyptian princess and made a treaty with Egypt; after the destruction of the First Temple, the prophet Jeremiah found Jewish colonies in Egypt; and a document discovered by archaeologists describes a Jewish colony in Elephantine, an island in the Nile, in the fifth century B.C.E.

After Alexander the Great conquered Egypt in 333 B.C.E., many Jewish immigrants came to live there and they prospered. Jews continued to live in Egypt throughout the centuries. Sometimes conditions were favorable for them and they lived in peace and prosperity. But other times they were discriminated against and life was hard.

In our time Egypt is a neighbor of the State of Israel. It is the only Arab country that has made peace with Israel. Although there are still many matters on which the two countries disagree, perhaps someday . these two nations that have shared many moments in history will live in complete peace and harmony with each other.

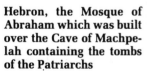

Hebron, the Mosque of Abraham which was built over the Cave of Machpelah containing the tombs of the Patriarchs

89

XIII
Israel in Egypt
Exodus 1:1–2:25

The descendants of Jacob, having grown in number, are enslaved by a Pharaoh "who knew not Joseph." They are cruelly oppressed and cry out to God for help.

Moses, the future liberator of the Israelites, is born and is adopted by the daughter of Pharaoh. He grows to manhood in the palace. When he learns of the plight of his people he is horrified and kills an Egyptian who is mistreating an Israelite. As a result, he becomes a fugitive and flees to the desert, where he is befriended by Jethro, a Midianite priest, marries Jethro's daughter, and becomes the father of a son.

Summary: EXODUS 1:1–13

The descendants of Jacob multiplied and increased very greatly in Egypt so that the land was filled with them.

A new king arose over Egypt	וַיָּקָם מֶלֶךְ־חָדָשׁ עַל־מִצְרָיִם
who did not know Joseph.	אֲשֶׁר לֹא־יָדַע אֶת־יוֹסֵף:

And he said to his people, "The Israelites are much too numerous for us. Let us deal shrewdly with them so that they will not increase; otherwise in the event of war they may join our enemies and fight against us."

So the Egyptians set taskmasters over the Israelites and forced them to do hard labor, and they built for Pharaoh the cities of Pithom and Rameses.

But the more they were oppressed, the more they increased, and the more the Egyptians feared them.

The Egyptians made life very difficult for the Israelite slaves. They forced them to do hard labor building structures of mortar and bricks and working in the fields.

But this was not enough for Pharaoh. He ordered that every Israelite baby boy be killed, but he allowed the girls to live.

Now there was a woman of the House of Levi who had a son. When she saw how beautiful he was, she hid him for three months. When she could hide him no longer she got a wicker basket and sealed it with pitch.

She put the child in it	וַתָּשֶׂם בָּה אֶת־הַיֶּלֶד
and placed it among the reeds	וַתָּשֶׂם בַּסּוּף
by the banks of the Nile.	עַל־שְׂפַת הַיְאֹר

The daughter of Pharaoh found the child and took pity on it. She made him her son and named him Moses, explaining, "I drew him out of the water."

COMMENTARIES

From the Midrash

One day Pharaoh dreamed that he was sitting on a throne. A man stood before him with a balance scale in his hands. On one side of the scale was a young lamb. On the other side were all the great men and nobles of Egypt. The side with the single lamb hung lower than the side of the scale with all the great men of Egypt.

Pharaoh called his wise men to interpret his dream. They told him that it meant that one day an Israelite child would be born who would destroy all of the land and its inhabitants and bring the Israelites out of Egypt.

Pharaoh was frightened. He wanted to protect himself from this danger. So he ordered all Israelite newborn boys put to death from that day on.

Pharaoh ordered that all newborn boys, both Israelite and Egyptian, should be killed. An astrologer had told him that the savior of the Israelites was about to be born, but had not said whether he would be an Israelite or an Egyptian. Pharaoh was so afraid that the Israelites would rise up against him if they were freed, and so eager to keep them as slaves because they were such valuable workers, that he ordered all male children killed.

Some time after, when Moses had grown up, he went out among the Israelites and saw how badly they were oppressed. He came upon an Egyptian beating a Hebrew. Moses looked all around him. When he saw no one, he killed the Egyptian and hid him in the sand. When Pharaoh learned of this he sought to kill Moses, but Moses fled from Pharaoh.

Moses ran away from Egypt and came to the land of Midian. There he sat down beside a well. The priest of Midian had seven daughters who came to draw water at the well. But shepherds came and drove them away.

Moses came to their defense	וַיָּקָם מֹשֶׁה וַיּוֹשִׁעָן
and watered their flock.	וַיַּשְׁקְ אֶת־צֹאנָם.

When they returned to their father and told him what had happened, he extended hospitality to Moses. Moses stayed in the home of the Midianite priest. He married the priest's daughter Zipporah, and became the father of a son, Gershom.

COMMENTARIES

From the Midrash

When Moses went out among the Israelites and saw their oppression, his heart went out to them. Although he had been raised as a prince and had never done any physical labor, he helped them complete their tasks like a common slave. When God saw this, He said, "Because you cast your lot with the Children of Israel in their time of sorrow and need, and gave up all the privileges of your high station, I shall also put aside all else in heaven and earth and speak only to you."

A long time after this the king of Egypt died. The Israelites suffered under the burdens of their slavery. They cried out to God for help. God heard their cries and remembered His covenant with Abraham.

God looked upon the Israelites,	וַיַּרְא אֱלֹהִים אֶת־בְּנֵי יִשְׂרָאֵל
and God took notice of them.	וַיֵּדַע אֱלֹהִים׃

COMMENTARIES

From the Midrash

When God wanted to find a compassionate leader to lead the Israelites out of Egypt and save them from slavery, He decided to test Moses. He watched Moses as he guarded his flock of sheep. As Moses tended the sheep, a young lamb separated itself from the rest of the flock and ran away. Moses pursued the lamb until it stopped at a waterhole to drink. The lamb was very young, and it had run very far. Moses worried that it was too weak to come back by itself. He gently lifted the lamb in his arms, held it against his body so it would not be afraid, and carried it all the way back to the flock.

When God saw the kindness and concern that Moses had for the lamb, God knew that Moses would be a kind and compassionate leader for the Children of Israel.

94

XIV

Moses

Exodus 3:1–4:18

Moses has a vision in which God speaks to him from a burning bush. The voice instructs him to go first to Pharaoh and then to the Israelites and make it known that God is ready to take the Israelites out of Egypt.

Moses doubts his ability, since he is "slow of speech and tongue," but God reassures him that, aided by his brother Aaron, he will be able to succeed.

Summary: EXODUS 3:1–12

One day, while tending the flocks of his father-in-law, Jethro, the priest of Midian, Moses came to Horeb, the Mountain of God. There he saw a bush that was all aflame but did not burn up. As he watched,

God called to him from the bush,	וַיִּקְרָא אֵלָיו אֱלֹהִים מִתּוֹךְ הַסְּנֶה
"Moses! Moses!"	וַיֹּאמֶר מֹשֶׁה מֹשֶׁה
and he answered, "Here I am!"	וַיֹּאמֶר הִנֵּנִי.

95

And God said, "Do not come any closer; remove your sandals from your feet. You are standing on holy ground. I am the God of your father, the God of Abraham, Isaac, and Jacob."

Moses hid his face, for he was afraid to look. God continued to speak, "I have seen the plight of My people, and I am aware of their suffering. I have come to rescue them from the Egyptians. I will send you to Pharaoh, and you shall free My people, the Israelites, from Egypt."

But Moses said to God, "Who am I that I should go to Pharaoh and free the Israelites from Egypt?"

And God said, "I will be with you, and when you have freed the people from Egypt, you will worship God at this mountain."

COMMENTARIES

From the Midrash

God spoke to Moses from a burning thornbush. The thornbush is a lowly, insignificant bush. God chose it as the means of making His appearance before Moses because He wanted Moses to know that nothing in nature, even the lowly thornbush, can exist without God's presence within it. Another reason for choosing the thornbush was to show Moses that just as he chose to suffer along with Israel, so God, too, chose to suffer by placing Himself within the stunted, thorny bush.

God said to Moses, "Assemble all the people and say to them, 'The Lord, the God of your ancestors, has appeared to me and has said to me that He has taken note of your suffering and has declared that He will take you out of Egypt and bring you to a land flowing with milk and honey.' Then go to the elders of Israel and with them go to the king of Egypt and say to him, 'The Lord, God of the Hebrews, showed Himself to us. Let us therefore go into the wilderness for three days to sacrifice to the Lord our God.' I shall stretch out My hand and work wonders, and then he will let you go."

Moses said, "What if the people do not believe me and do not listen to me?"

God said to him, "What is that in your hand?" and he replied, "It is a rod."

God said, "Throw it on the ground."

Moses did, and it became a snake.

Then God said, "Put out your hand and pick it up by the tail."

Moses did, and it became a rod once more.

God said, "That is so that they may believe that the Lord, the God of your ancestors, did indeed appear to you."

Then the Lord said further, "Put your hand in your bosom." Moses did, and when he took it out it was encrusted with scales. "Those signs will prove that God has spoken to you," God said. "And if they do not believe those signs, then take some water from the Nile and pour it on the ground, and it will turn to blood."

But Moses said to God, "I have never been a man of words. I am slow of speech and slow of tongue."

And the Lord said to him,	וַיֹּאמֶר יְהֹוָה אֵלָיו
"Who gives man speech?	מִי שָׂם פֶּה לָאָדָם
Who makes him dumb or deaf,	אוֹ מִי־יָשׂוּם אִלֵּם אוֹ חֵרֵשׁ
seeing or blind?	אוֹ פִּקֵּחַ אוֹ עִוֵּר
Is it not I, the Lord?	הֲלֹא אָנֹכִי יְהֹוָה.

Now go, and I will be with you as you speak, and I will tell you what to say. Your brother Aaron will help you. You shall speak to him and put the words in his mouth, and I will be with you and tell you both what to do."

COMMENTARIES

From the Midrash

When Moses was a small child and lived in the palace of the king, he would often play with Pharaoh. One day, as he was playing, he took the king's crown from his head. Moses placed the crown on his own head. The king's advisors were very concerned. "One day this child will grow up and take your crown and become king in your stead," they said. "It would be best to have the child killed before he becomes a threat to the king."

But the king did not believe that Moses was a threat to him. "He is just a child," he said. "The crown is bright, and he was attracted to it. I will test him."

The king put before Moses the crown and a hot, brightly burning coal. If Moses went for the bright coal, the king would know that he was attracted to bright objects. But if he reached for the crown, the king would know that Moses would someday try to displace him as king.

Moses looked at the two objects. He reached for the crown. But as he put out his hand, an angel pushed his hand to the hot coal. Moses burned his hand and put it into his mouth to cool it. But a piece of the coal stuck to the hand. Moses burned his tongue. Although his life was saved, from that time on Moses was slow of speech and slow of tongue.

LEARNING MORE ABOUT:
BIBLE TRANSLATIONS

The first translation of the Bible into a foreign language was the Septuagint Bible. It was a translation of the Bible into Greek, written for the Jews of Alexandria, Egypt, at the beginning of the third century B.C.E. The word "Septuagint" means "seventy" in Greek. There is a legend that the seventy greatest scholars of that time were asked to translate the Bible from Hebrew into Greek. The scholars were isolated from each other for the entire time that they were doing the translation, and each one did his own translation. When they had finished, all seventy translations were exactly alike, word for word.

The Latin Vulgate Bible of 382 C.E. was the first major translation of the Bible into a Western European language. The Vulgate became the official Bible of the Roman Catholic Church.

The Bible was soon translated into hundreds of languages. Some were for Christian readers. Others, like the translations of Onkelos, Jonathan ben Uziel, and Saadia Gaon, were for Jews who could not read and understand Hebrew.

The Bible has been translated into 1,108 different languages. Wherever people live it is read and studied. For many hundreds of years it has been the all-time "best-seller" all over the world.

XV
Let My People Go

Exodus 4:19–12:51

Moses sets out with his family to return to Egypt. Together with Aaron he brings the message to the Israelites that God will redeem them. The brothers then go to Pharaoh, but their message is rejected—Pharaoh will not let the Israelites leave Egypt.

God punishes Pharaoh and the Egyptians with ten terrible plagues. Pharaoh relents, and the Israelites are liberated. They leave Egypt in such great haste that they are unable to bake bread in the usual manner by allowing it to rise, and so they bake flat cakes of unleavened bread as their food for the journey.

Summary: EXODUS 4:19–7:13

God said to Moses, "Return to Egypt, for all who sought to kill you are dead. Show Pharaoh the wonders I have put in your power and say, 'Let my people go.'"

Then God said to Aaron, "Go meet Moses in the wilderness." And Aaron did.

Together Moses and Aaron went to Pharaoh and said, "Thus says the Lord, God of Israel,

'Let My people	שַׁלַּח אֶת־עַמִּי
go that they may celebrate a festival to Me	וְיָחֹגּוּ לִי
in the wilderness.'"	בַּמִּדְבָּר:

But Pharaoh would not let the Israelites leave Egypt. Instead he instructed the taskmasters to make the burden of the Israelites even harder by not providing them with the straw necessary to make bricks. The Israelites were forced to find enough straw by themselves to meet their daily quota of bricks.

The Israelites were even more oppressed than before. They complained to Moses and held him responsible for their worsened condition.

COMMENTARIES

From the Midrash

When Moses saw how much the Israelites were suffering in Egypt, he spoke to God and said, "I have read Genesis and learned of the doom that befell the generation of the flood. It was a just judgment. And I have read of the Tower of Babel and how the languages were confused. That was also a just judgment. So was the punishment of the people of Sodom. But what has this nation, Israel, done that was so terrible that You allow it to suffer so much?"

God knew that Moses had spoken out of compassion for his brothers. He did not punish Moses for having so little faith. Instead He answered, "You will see what I will do to Pharaoh."

The Lord said to Moses, "Pharaoh is stubborn. He refuses to let My people go. Go to Pharaoh and say, 'The Lord God sent me to you to ask that His people may go to worship in the wilderness. But you did not allow them to go. Therefore, God will send a sign.'"

Then God told Moses to go to Aaron and tell Aaron to hold out his arm over the waters of Egypt. Aaron did, and all the bodies of water in Egypt turned to blood. There was blood throughout the land of Egypt. But still Pharaoh would not let the Israelites go.

Then God sent more disasters to plague Egypt. The land swarmed with frogs. The dust of the earth turned to lice. Swarms of insects invaded the country, but the region of Goshen, where the Israelites lived, did not have insects. All the livestock belonging to the Egyptians was struck by disease and died—but not a single head of the livestock of Israel died. Boils covered the bodies of men and beasts. But still Pharaoh did not let the Israelites go.

Still more plagues were sent by God. Hail, heavier than had ever been seen, fell, and every person or animal that was outside perished. But in Goshen, where the Israelites were, there was no hail. Locusts came and ate up all the grass. Three days of darkness descended on the land.

People could not see one another,	לֹא־רָאוּ אִישׁ אֶת־אָחִיו
and for three days no one could get up from where he was;	וְלֹא־קָמוּ אִישׁ מִתַּחְתָּיו שְׁלֹשֶׁת יָמִים
but all the Israelites	וּלְכָל־בְּנֵי יִשְׂרָאֵל
enjoyed light in their homes.	הָיָה אוֹר בְּמוֹשְׁבֹתָם.

But still Pharaoh would not let the Israelites go.

COMMENTARIES

From the Midrash

The plagues sent by God to punish the Egyptians corresponded to cruel actions of the Egyptians against the Israelites. Because the Israelites were forced to draw water for the Egyptians, the water was changed to blood. Because the Egyptians forced the Israelites to catch fish for them, the rivers were filled with frogs. Because the Israelites were forced to sweep the Egyptian houses, the dust of the air was changed to lice. Because the Egyptians forced the Israelites to take care of their sheep, the sheep were struck down by disease, and so on. The tenth plague, the killing of the firstborn, was a punishment for Pharaoh's order to murder the boy children of the Israelites at their birth.

Then God said to Moses, "I will send one more plague against Pharaoh and the Egyptians, and he will let you go from here. Tell the people to get ready to leave Egypt.

Toward midnight	כַּחֲצֹת הַלַּיְלָה
I will go forth among the Egyptians,	אֲנִי יוֹצֵא בְּתוֹךְ מִצְרָיִם.
and every firstborn in the land of Egypt shall die.	וּמֵת כָּל בְּכוֹר בְּאֶרֶץ מִצְרָיִם.

"From the firstborn of the Pharaoh to the firstborn of the slave girl, all shall die. And there shall be a loud cry in the land, and all the courtiers of Egypt shall come and say, 'Leave—you and all the people who follow you.'"

COMMENTARIES

When Moses announced the last plague, he closed with the words, "All Pharaoh's servants shall bow down to me and plead with me to take the Israelites out of Egypt." Moses knew that Pharaoh, too, would bow to him and plead with him to leave and take the Israelites. But he mentioned only the servants of the king and not the king himself because he never forgot the respect that was due to a ruler.

SOMETHING TO THINK ABOUT

Do you agree that a ruler (or a person who holds high office) is entitled to respect even when he/she is wrong? Why? (American historians tell us that when General Lee surrendered to General Grant after the Civil War, Grant showed his respect for Lee by not accepting the sword that Lee surrendered.)

COMMENTARIES

From the Midrash

Most of the Egyptians did not believe that the God of Israel would really kill all the firstborn Egyptians. But those who did believe it sent their children to the homes of Israelite neighbors so that they would be spared. But in the morning, when the Israelites woke up, they found the dead bodies of the Egyptian children.

Not only the firstborn Egyptian children were killed, but also the firstborn of the cattle. Since the Egyptians worshipped animals, God wanted them to see how powerless their gods were.

The hyssop was chosen for the Passover ceremony because it is the lowliest of plants. God wanted Israel to know that although they are as lowly as the hyssop, they are bound together like a bunch of hyssop and are God's special treasure.

The Israelites prepared to leave Egypt. Moses called the elders together and instructed them to pick out lambs for their families and prepare the Passover offering. First each family was to slaughter a lamb from the flock. Then they were to dip a bunch of hyssop in the blood and apply the blood to the doorposts. That night, they were not to leave their homes.

In the middle of the night God struck down all the firstborn in the homes of Egypt. But when God saw the blood on the doorposts of the Israelite homes, He passed over them, and the Israelites were spared.

Then God said,

This day shall be a memorial for you.	וְהָיָה הַיּוֹם הַזֶּה לָכֶם לְזִכָּרוֹן
You shall celebrate it as a festival to the Lord throughout all your generations	וְחַגֹּתֶם אֹתוֹ חַג לַיהֹוָה לְדֹרֹתֵיכֶם
It is an eternal commandment that you shall celebrate it.	חֻקַּת עוֹלָם תְּחָגֻּהוּ.

That night, Pharaoh called Moses and Aaron and said, "Leave Egypt—you and the Israelites! Go worship the Lord as you said."

The Israelites left in a great hurry. They took the dough they were preparing before it leavened, and they baked unleavened cakes of the dough, because they left Egypt in such a hurry that they had not prepared food for the journey.

LEARNING MORE ABOUT:
THE PASSOVER CELEBRATION

In ancient times the Israelites celebrated Passover by sacrificing a lamb and then eating the roasted lamb with maror (bitter herbs) and matza. This ceremony has evolved through the ages into the beautiful and elaborate home ritual we call the Seder. The Hebrew word *seder* means "order." It is so-called because we proceed through the various steps of the ceremony in a prescribed order which is celebrated by Jews all over the world. This is the "order," or *seder,* we follow:

1. *Kaddesh:* Recite the Kiddush over the wine.   1. קַדֵּשׁ.
2. *R'chatz:* Wash hands.   2. וּרְחַץ.
3. *Karpas:* Eat the parsley dipped in saltwater; say the blessing.   3. כַּרְפַּס.
4. *Yachatz:* Break the middle matza. Hide one part. It must be eaten at the end of the Seder, so whoever finds it gets a prize.   4. יַחַץ.
5. *Maggid:* Read the story of Passover from the Haggadah.   5. מַגִּיד.
6. *Rachtzah:* Wash hands.   6. רָחְצָה.
7. *Motzi Matza:* Recite blessing over the matza and eat the matza.   7. מוֹצִיא, מַצָּה.
8. *Maror:* Bitter herbs.   8. מָרוֹר.
9. *Korech:* Combine matza, maror, and charoset, and eat together.   9. כּוֹרֵךְ.
10. *Shulchan orech:* Eat dinner.   10. שֻׁלְחָן עוֹרֵךְ.
11. *Zaffun:* End the meal by eating the afikomen.   11. צָפוּן.
12. *Barech:* Say Grace after meals.   12. בָּרֵךְ.
13. *Hallel:* Recite Hallel.   13. הַלֵּל.
14. *Nirza:* End the service.   14. נִרְצָה.

LEARNING MORE ABOUT:
THE EXODUS FROM EGYPT

Archaeologists, historians, and Bible scholars have always been interested in learning more about the Exodus. They have been concerned with such questions as: Who was the Pharaoh of the Exodus? When did the Exodus take place? What route did the Israelites follow? and so on. They have found the answers to some of these questions.

On the basis of historical and archaeological evidence, most scholars believe that the Exodus took place about 1290 B.C.E. (about 3,300 years ago) and that Rameses II was the Pharaoh of the Exodus. Here are some of the reasons they give:

1. The Bible tells us that the Hebrews lived in Goshen, close to the Pharaoh's palace. This is in the Nile Delta region of Egypt. Historians have learned that Pharaoh Rameses II built his capital in the Nile Delta.

2. The Bible tells us that the Hebrews built the store-cities of Pithom and Rameses for the Pharaoh. Archaeologists have found these cities. The city of Rameses was originally called Avaris, but in 1300 B.C.E. it was rebuilt by Rameses II and renamed after himself.

3. Archaeologists have excavated some of the ancient cities of Canaan. These excavations have shown that in the period several decades after 1290 B.C.E., many of the cities underwent much destruction, apparently from a war. This date is in keeping with the Biblical account of the conquest of Canaan by the Children of Israel, which began under the leadership of Joshua after their forty years of wandering in the desert.

An Egyptian brick with the imprint of Pharaoh Rameses II. Rameses II was probably the Pharaoh of the Exodus.

XVI

The Exodus

Moses instructs the Israelites on how to observe the festival of Passover, and they proceed on their journey.

Pharaoh has a change of heart and pursues the fleeing Israelites, but they escape when the Sea of Reeds opens for them. The sea closes again, and all the pursuing Egyptians are drowned.

Moses and the Children of Israel sing a song of victory in which they praise God and thank Him for having saved them from the Egyptians.

Summary: EXODUS 13:1–16

Moses said to the people, "Remember this day that you were freed from slavery in Egypt, and do not eat any unleavened bread on it. When the Lord brings you into the land promised to your ancestors—a land flowing with milk and honey—you shall observe a festival in this month in the following manner: You shall eat unleavened bread for seven days, and you shall explain to your children,

'It is because of what the Lord did for me	בַּעֲבוּר זֶה עָשָׂה יְהֹוָה לִי
when I went free from Egypt.'	בְּצֵאתִי מִמִּצְרָיִם:

And you shall place a sign on your hand and a reminder on your forehead to remember the teachings of the Lord and that He brought you out of the land of Egypt.

And when you arrive in the land that was promised to you, you shall set aside for the Lord every firstborn of your sheep for a sacrifice."

FOCUS ON:
BIBLICAL SELECTIONS IN THE PRAYERBOOK

The following selection from Exodus 13 is recited after putting on tefillin.

God spoke to Moses, saying:	וַיְדַבֵּר יְהֹוָה אֶל מֹשֶׁה לֵּאמֹר׃
"Dedicate to me every first-born amongst the Israelites, human being and animal it is mine."	קַדֶּשׁ־לִי כָל בְּכוֹר פֶּטֶר כָּל רֶחֶם בִּבְנֵי יִשְׂרָאֵל בָּאָדָם וּבַבְּהֵמָה, לִי הוּא׃
And Moses said to the people:	וַיֹּאמֶר מֹשֶׁה אֶל הָעָם,
"Remember this day	זָכוֹר אֶת הַיּוֹם הַזֶּה
on which you left Egypt	אֲשֶׁר יְצָאתֶם מִמִּצְרַיִם
where you were enslaved	מִבֵּית עֲבָדִים,
and how God freed you with a mighty hand.	כִּי בְּחֹזֶק יָד הוֹצִיא יְהֹוָה אֶתְכֶם מִזֶּה,
Do not eat any unleavened bread on it.	וְלֹא יֵאָכֵל חָמֵץ׃
This day in the month of Aviv you are going free."	הַיּוֹם אַתֶּם יֹצְאִים, בְּחֹדֶשׁ הָאָבִיב.

From the Talmud

Rabbi Aba Arika (Rab), a student of Judah the Prince, was so righteous that he would not walk even four cubits without a scroll of the Torah and without wearing tefillin on his hand and on his forehead.

Summary: EXODUS 13:17–14:31

The Israelites left Egypt and journeyed into the wilderness. Moses carried with him the bones of Joseph to be buried in Canaan, as Joseph's children had promised to do many years before. God went before them as a pillar of fire by night to give them light, and as a cloud by day.

Now when the king of Egypt learned that the Israelites had left, he had a change of heart and said,

"What is this we have done,	מַה־זֹּאת עָשִׂינוּ
releasing Israel	כִּי־שִׁלַּחְנוּ אֶת־יִשְׂרָאֵל
from our service?"	מֵעָבְדֵנוּ.

Pharaoh took chariots and officers and pursued the Israelites. He overtook them on the shores of the Sea of Reeds, where they had made their camp. As Pharaoh and the Egyptians came close, the Israelites saw them and were afraid. They cried out to Moses, "Did you bring us out of Egypt to die in the wilderness?"

Moses held out his arm over the sea, and God caused the waters to part and form a wall on either side of the seabed. The Israelites walked through on dry land.

The Egyptians, seeing the dry land, tried to follow. But when all the Israelites had finished crossing, Moses held out his arm once more and the waters returned as they had been. Pharaoh's entire army drowned in the waters of the Sea of Reeds.

COMMENTARIES

From the Midrash

The sea did not part as soon as the Israelites stepped into it. It did not part until they were in water up to their nostrils and in danger of drowning. God did this to test the faith of the people.

Pharaoh was the last Egyptian to drown in the waters of the Sea of Reeds. It was part of his punishment to witness the death of all his soldiers and servants before he himself was allowed to die.

From the Talmud

When the angels witnessed the wonderful miracle of God in parting the waters of the Sea of Reeds so that the Israelites could cross on dry land while the Egyptians drowned, they began to sing happy songs of praise to God. But God did not allow them to rejoice. "The Egyptians are also My creations," He said. "Do not sing while My creatures are dying."

FOCUS ON:
BIBLICAL SELECTIONS IN THE PRAYERBOOK

The following selection is from Exodus 14 and is in the Morning Service (Shacharit).

God delivered Israel that day	וַיּוֹשַׁע יְהוָה בַּיּוֹם הַהוּא אֶת יִשְׂרָאֵל
from the Egyptians,	מִיַּד מִצְרָיִם.
and Israel saw	וַיַּרְא יִשְׂרָאֵל
the Egyptians dead on the shores of the sea.	אֶת מִצְרַיִם מֵת עַל שְׂפַת הַיָּם.
When Israel saw the great power	וַיַּרְא יִשְׂרָאֵל אֶת הַיָּד הַגְּדֹלָה,
which God had exercised against the Egyptians,	אֲשֶׁר עָשָׂה יְהוָה בְּמִצְרָיִם.
the people feared God.	וַיִּירְאוּ הָעָם אֶת יְהוָה,
They had faith in God	וַיַּאֲמִינוּ בַּיהוָה
and God's servant, Moses.	וּבְמֹשֶׁה עַבְדּוֹ.

Summary: EXODUS 15:1–21

The Israelites praised God and sang a song of victory:

I will sing to the Lord,	אָשִׁירָה לַיהוָֹה
For He has triumphed.	כִּי־גָאֹה גָּאָה
He has drowned horse and driver	סוּס וְרֹכְבוֹ רָמָה
In the sea.	בַיָּם
I will praise Him.	וְאַנְוֵהוּ
Who is like You	מִי־כָמֹכָה
Among the mighty, O Lord?	בָּאֵלִים יְהוָֹה
Who is like You,	מִי כָּמֹכָה
Great in holiness?	נֶאְדָּר בַּקֹּדֶשׁ
The Lord will rule forever and ever.	יְהוָֹה יִמְלֹךְ לְעֹלָם וָעֶד

COMMENTARIES

From the Midrash

Before God saved the Israelites He did many other great things. He saved Abraham from destruction in a fiery furnace. He saved Isaac from being slaughtered and sacrificed. He saved Jacob from Esau. But no one else sang songs of praise to God. When the Israelites were saved, they sang to God. God listened and said, "I have been waiting for this."

FOCUS ON:
BIBLICAL SELECTIONS IN THE PRAYERBOOK

The following selections from the Morning Service (Shacharit) were taken from Exodus 15.

Who is like you among the mighty, O Eternal?	מִי כָמְכָה בָּאֵלִים יְהֹוָה?
Who is like You, great in holiness,	מִי כָּמְכָה נֶאְדָּר בַּקֹּדֶשׁ?
Awesome in splendor, doing wonders?	נוֹרָא תְהִלֹּת עֹשֵׂה־פֶלֶא:
The Eternal will rule forever and ever.	יְהֹוָה יִמְלֹךְ לְעוֹלָם וָעֶד.

XVII

In the Desert

Exodus 15:22–18:27

The Israelites leave the Sea of Reeds and travel in the desert wilderness. They experience shortages of food and water and complain to Moses and Aaron. But God takes care of their needs. He provides water to drink and manna and quail to eat.

Jethro, priest of Midian, hears of Moses' role in leading the Israelites from Egypt and joins Moses in the wilderness. He brings with him Zipporah, Moses' wife, and the two sons of Moses and Zipporah.

Jethro observes Moses in his function as judge and offers some well-received advice.

Summary: EXODUS 15:22–16:36

Moses led the Israelites from the Sea of Reeds into the desert wilderness. They camped in Marah but could not drink the water there because it was bitter. The people grumbled to Moses, and he cried out to the Lord. God showed Moses a piece of wood and told him to throw it into the water. Moses did, and the water became sweet.

As they continued traveling, the Israelites complained to Moses because there was no food and they were hungry. They longed to be back in Egypt. There, at least, they were well fed. God heard their grumbling. He rained down manna from the sky. Each day enough manna fell to satisfy their needs for that day. But on the sixth day, a double portion rained down so that they would not have to gather food on Shabbat.

COMMENTARIES

From the Midrash

Manna was a wonderful food. It did not have a taste of its own but tasted different to each person who ate it. Whatever a person's favorite food was, that is how the manna tasted to him.

From Rashi

The Israelites cried out for bread and meat. But God promised them only that they would have enough bread (manna). Bread is a necessity, but meat is a luxury.

From Ibn Ezra

The waters at Marah were not really bitter. The Israelites felt bitter, and so everything they tasted was bitter to them.

The Israelites then set up camp at Rephidim. There they were attacked by the Amalekites. Moses appointed Joshua to pick some men and do battle with the Amalekites. Moses stationed himself on the top of a nearby hill. In his hand he held the rod that God had given him. When Moses held up his hand, the Israelites battled victoriously. But when Moses lowered his hand, the Israelites lost ground.

Moses stood on the hill above the battle with his arms raised. But after a while his arms got tired and he could no longer hold them up. His hands began to drop. Aaron placed a stone on the ground for Moses to sit on. Then Aaron and Hur held up Moses' arms until the battle was over. the Amalekites were defeated.

COMMENTARIES

From the Midrash

Although it seemed that victory or defeat depended on whether or not Moses held his arms up, this was not really so. When the Israelites looked at Moses and saw him standing with his arms up, they thought of God and heaven, and the battle went well for them. It was their lofty thoughts that won the battle.

Jethro, priest of Midian and Moses' father-in-law, heard all that God had done for Moses and for Israel, his people. So Jethro took Zipporah, Moses' wife, and her two sons and brought them to Moses in the wilderness.

Moses went out to greet his father-in-law. He told him everything that the Lord had done to Pharaoh and to the Egyptians for Israel's sake —

all the hardships	אֵת כָּל־הַתְּלָאָה
that had befallen them on the way,	אֲשֶׁר מְצָאָתַם בַּדֶּרֶךְ
and how the Lord had delivered them.	וַיַּצִּלֵם יְהֹוָה.

Jethro rejoiced over the kindness that God had shown Israel and said, "Blessed be the Lord. Now I know that the Lord is greater than all the other gods."

The next day Jethro observed Moses as he sat as a judge over his people. When Jethro saw how much Moses had to do, he said, "The thing you are doing is not right. You represent the people before God, and you make known to them what they are to do and the practices they are to follow. Seek among the people capable men and set them as chiefs over thousands, hundreds, fifties, and tens, and let them judge the people at all times. Let them bring only the major disputes to you, but let them decide the minor disputes themselves."

Moses listened to his father-in-law and did just as he had said.

COMMENTARIES

From the Midrash

When Jethro saw all that God had done for the Israelites, he said, "Blessed is the Lord." Jethro was not an Israelite, but he helped to turn the Israelites to God. Sometimes it takes a non-Jew to turn us to God.

From the Talmud

Jethro sought to lighten Moses' work because judging was a more difficult task than leading the people from Egypt. A judge has a very great responsibility. He has the power to change people's lives. Therefore a judge must always pass judgment as if a sword were suspended over him.

LEARNING MORE ABOUT BIBLICAL COMMENTARIES: NACHMANIDES

Nachmanides was born in Gerona, Spain. He was one of the outstanding Bible commentators of the Middle Ages. In 1267 he settled in Jerusalem. From there he moved to Acre, where he established a Talmudic academy.

Nachmanides was a physician by profession, but he was recognized as the foremost expert of his time on Jewish law. His commentary on the Bible was highly regarded by scholars for its wise interpretations based on logic and knowledge of Jewish law. The interpretations and commentaries of Nachmanides are still studied by students of the Bible all over the world to help them understand the deeper meaning of the text.

Nachmanides is often referred to as Ramban, an abbreviation of his full name in Hebrew: Rabbi Moses ben Nachman.

XVIII
Revelation at Sinai

Exodus 19:1–23:33

The Children of Israel arrive at Mount Sinai, where God reveals Himself to them. Moses ascends Sinai and receives the Ten Commandments and other laws by which Israel is to live.

Summary: EXODUS 19:1–25

On the third new moon after their departure from Egypt, the Israelites entered the Sinai desert. There God called to Moses from the mountain and commanded him to say to the Israelites, "If you obey Me faithfully and keep My covenant, you shall be My treasured possession among all the peoples.

| You shall be to Me a kingdom of priests | וְאַתֶּם תִּהְיוּ־לִי מַמְלֶכֶת כֹּהֲנִים |
| and a holy nation." | וְגוֹי קָדוֹשׁ. |

Moses called the people together and told them what God had commanded him. And all the people responded as one, "All that the Lord has spoken we will do!"

Then God said to Moses, "Tell the people to stay pure today and tomorrow and to wash their clothes. On the third day I will appear. Warn the people not to touch the mountain, for whoever touches the mountain will die. When the shofar sounds a long blast they may go up to the mountain."

Moses told the people all that God had said. On the third day there was thunder and lightning and a dense cloud on the mountain. Soon a shofar blast was heard, and the people trembled. Moses led the people out of the camp, and they stood at the foot of the mountain.

Mount Sinai was covered with smoke, for the Lord had come down upon it in fire. The whole mountain trembled violently. The sound of the shofar got louder and louder. God called to Moses from the top of the mountain, and Moses went up to hear the words of God.

COMMENTARIES

From the Midrash

The Torah was given in the wilderness of Sinai rather than in the land of Israel. This teaches us that it is a law for all nations. If it had been given in Israel, the other nations could say that Israel alone is obligated to obey its laws.

God did not give the Torah to the Israelites until they were able to stand as one at the foot of Mount Sinai. God waited until they were of one heart and mind, and there was peace among them.

From the Vilna Gaon

No one can observe all the laws of the Torah. There are some laws that can be observed only by landowners, others only by priests, and so on. It is only the Jewish people *as a whole* that can fulfill all the commandments.

God spoke all these words saying:

I am the Lord your God who brought you out of the land of Egypt, out of the house of bondage.

You shall have no other gods beside Me.

You shall not take the name of the Lord in vain.

Remember the Sabbath to keep it holy.

Honor your father and your mother.

You shall not murder.

You shall not be unfaithful to wife or husband.

You shall not steal.

You shall not bear false witness.

You shall not desire what is your neighbor's.

וַיְדַבֵּר אֱלֹהִים אֵת כָּל־הַדְּבָרִים הָאֵלֶּה לֵאמֹר

אָנֹכִי יְהֹוָה אֱלֹהֶיךָ אֲשֶׁר הוֹצֵאתִיךָ מֵאֶרֶץ מִצְרַיִם מִבֵּית עֲבָדִים

לֹא־יִהְיֶה לְךָ אֱלֹהִים אֲחֵרִים עַל פָּנַי

לֹא תִשָּׂא אֶת־שֵׁם־יְהֹוָה לַשָּׁוְא

זָכוֹר אֶת־יוֹם הַשַּׁבָּת לְקַדְּשׁוֹ

כַּבֵּד אֶת־אָבִיךָ וְאֶת אִמֶּךָ

לֹא תִּרְצָח

לֹא תִּנְאָף

לֹא תִּגְנֹב

לֹא־תַעֲנֶה בְרֵעֲךָ עֵד שָׁקֶר

לֹא תַחְמֹד אֵשֶׁת רֵעֶךָ

COMMENTARIES

From the Midrash

When God gave the law to the Israelites, He said, "If you will obey My commandments, I will reward you by allowing you to enter the world-to-come."

"But will we have no reward in this life?" asked the people.

"I will give you Shabbat," said the Lord. "It will give you a small taste of Paradise."

All prophecies and all future teachings were also handed down on Mount Sinai.

When God gave the Torah, no bird sang, no fowl flew, the sea did not roar, and no creature spoke. Even the angels stopped singing their praises of God. The entire world was silent. Only the voice of God could be heard, saying, "I am the Lord your God."

From Rashi

In order not to have the people think that one commandment was more important than another, God spoke all the commandments at one time.

FOCUS ON:
BIBLICAL SELECTIONS IN THE PRAYERBOOK

This line from the Shabbat Morning Kiddush is from Exodus 20.

So did God bless	עַל כֵּן בֵּרַךְ יְהֹוָה
the seventh day	אֶת יוֹם הַשַּׁבָּת
and make it holy.	וַיְקַדְּשֵׁהוּ.

After God had spoken to Moses and given him the Ten Commandments, He continued to make His laws known to Moses. He commanded Moses regarding laws which related to worship and to sacrifices. But many of the laws concerned people and how they must behave to one another and the obligations that one person has to another. Some of the laws were:

"If you have a Hebrew slave, you must set him free after six years. If he has a wife, she, too, must be freed, so that she can leave with him. But if the slave does not wish to go free, he will remain a slave forever."

"One who fatally strikes another shall be put to death. But if the death is accidental, the striker may flee to a place of refuge."

"A kidnapper shall be put to death."

"Take an eye for an eye, a tooth for a tooth, a hand for a hand, a foot for a foot, a burn for a burn, a wound for a wound, a bruise for a bruise."

"If an ox gores a person to death, the ox shall be killed, but the owner shall not be punished. But if the ox is in the habit of goring, and its owner knows and fails to guard it, then the owner, too, shall be put to death."

"If a person steals an ox or a sheep and slaughters it or sells it, he shall pay back five oxen or four sheep. But if the stolen ox or sheep is found alive in his possession, he shall pay back only double."

"You shall not wrong a stranger or oppress him, for you were strangers in the land of Egypt."

"You shall not mistreat a widow or an orphan."

"You must not carry false rumors."

"Do not take bribes."

"You shall serve the Lord your God, and He will bless you."

COMMENTARIES

From the Midrash

The commandments and laws which God gave to Israel were given in great detail. That was because Israel was very dear to God. It is like a father who has a child who is very dear to him. He does not want the child to hurt himself, so he gives him very detailed instructions about what to do and where to go.

From Rashi

Not only the Ten Commandments but also the civil laws that follow were issued by God on Mount Sinai.

The real meaning of "an eye for an eye" is not that an offender should have his own limbs taken away in retribution, but that the offender must pay the value of the eye or the tooth which he destroyed or injured. This is determined by how much less an injured man would be worth in the slave market without the injured part.

From Maimonides

It is especially important to treat widows and orphans with kindness, since they are often depressed and unhappy. Not only a poor widow or orphan should be treated kindly, but even the widow or orphan of a king must be given special consideration.

Nahmanides' synagogue in Jerusalem. From the *Casale Pilgrim*, a sixteenth century guide to the holy places of Palestine.

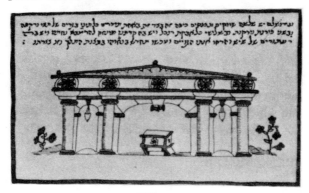

125

FOCUS ON THE CONCEPT:
AN EYE FOR AN EYE

The Bible, in Exodus 21:24–25 and Leviticus 24:17–19, describes a law of retaliation which allows a person who has been injured by another to get even in kind. The law says, "If a person has injured his neighbor, it shall be done to him as he has done—fracture for fracture, eye for eye, tooth for tooth."

The law of retaliation is a law that was followed by many ancient peoples in the Middle East. The Talmud interpreted this law to mean that a victim could collect a money fine from one who had injured him, rather than actually injure the one who did him harm. The Talmudic law worked out a table of fines to compensate the victim. If the offense resulted in injury or illness, then the victim could collect for loss of earning power, medical treatment, and other expenses.

This Talmudic explanation of the law has come down to our own time in the civil law of our country. If one person injures another because of negligence, or because he meant to, the victim may sue and collect money damages from the person who has injured him. This may include compensation for loss of earning power, medical treatment, and other expenses.

XIX

The Covenant

Exodus 24:1–31:18

Moses is called by God to ascend Mount Sinai. He stays on the mountain for forty days and nights and is instructed in the law. Moses also receives specific instructions for the construction of a sanctuary, or Tabernacle, to house the tablets on which the law will be inscribed.

God establishes the Sabbath as a sign of the covenant between Israel and God. Moses is given the two stone tablets of the covenant inscribed by the hand of God.

Summary: EXODUS 24:1–18

Moses repeated to the people all that God had commanded,

and the people answered as one,	וַיַּעַן כָּל־הָעָם קוֹל אֶחָד
"All the things that the Lord commanded	וַיֹּאמְרוּ כָּל־הַדְּבָרִים אֲשֶׁר־דִּבֶּר יְהוָֹה
we will do."	נַעֲשֶׂה.

Then God said to Moses, "Come up to Me on the mountain and wait there, and I will give you some stone tablets with the teachings and commandments which I have inscribed."

127

Moses and his attendant, Joshua, approached the mountain where God was. A cloud covered the mountain and hid it for six days. On the seventh day God called to Moses from the midst of the cloud. And God appeared as a fire on top of the mountain.

Moses went inside the cloud and went up to the top of the mountain. There he stayed for forty days and forty nights.

COMMENTARIES

From the Midrash

The people answered as one, "All the things that the Lord commanded we will do." Before God, all the people were alike. None were more important or less important in His eyes.

When Moses called the people together to teach them the law, they said, "We will do and we will listen." Moses asked, "How can you promise to do the commandments before you hear what they are?" The people answered him, "We will do whatever we hear from God."

God spoke to Moses, saying, "Let the people make a sanctuary for Me that I may live among you. Ask the people to bring gifts of gold and silver and other precious things, and make the Tabernacle and its furnishings exactly as I show you. Make an ark as I instruct you, with poles to carry it, and put in the ark the tablets which I will give you. Then have the Israelites bring clear oil of beaten olives and place it in lamps in the sanctuary which shall be kindled regularly.

"Aaron and his sons will serve Me in the sanctuary as My priests. They will wear special vestments when they enter the sanctuary or officiate in its rituals."

COMMENTARIES

From the Midrash

God ordered that the sanctuary was to be built from acacia wood. The acacia tree is a non-fruit-bearing tree. God wanted to set an example for all time that the wood of fruit-bearing trees should not be used for building.

From the Talmud

God ordered that the ark was to be covered inside and outside with gold. This was to teach us that if a person just seems wise on the outside, he is not really wise. He must be wise inside as well.

LEARNING MORE ABOUT:
THE TABERNACLE

The tablets of the covenant which contained the Ten Commandments were kept in an ark which was placed in a sanctuary called the Tabernacle (Mishkan). According to the Bible, the Tabernacle, also called the Tent of Meeting, was built by the Israelites in the wilderness after the Exodus from Egypt. It was a portable tent about 45 feet long, 15 feet wide, and 36 feet high. At the back of the tent was a small room curtained off from the rest of the area. This was called the Holy of Holies. Here was kept the ark with the tablets.

The Tabernacle is described in great detail in the Bible. The front part of the tent was enclosed by wooden columns from which hung blue, purple, and scarlet hangings. In front of the Holy of Holies, and separated from it by a curtain, was another holy area with a table, bread, seven-branched menorah, and golden altar. In the front courtyard there was a copper altar and a copper basin where the priests washed before they brought the sacrifices on the altar.

After the Israelites settled in Canaan, the Tabernacle rested at Shiloh in the center of the country. When Jerusalem became the capital city of Israel in the time of King David, a new sanctuary was built on Mount Zion, and the holy ark was brought there. This was the central place of worship for the nation until King Solomon built the Holy Temple (Bet Hamikdash), which became Israel!'s permanent sanctuary.

Then the Lord said to Moses, "Instruct the Israelites to keep My Sabbaths. It will be a sign between Me and you forever.

Six days work may be done,	שֵׁשֶׁת יָמִים יֵעָשֶׂה מְלָאכָה
but on the seventh day there shall be a Sabbath of complete rest,	וּבַיּוֹם הַשְּׁבִיעִי שַׁבַּת שַׁבָּתוֹן
holy to the Lord.	קֹדֶשׁ לַיהֹוָה.

The Sabbath shall be a sign for all time between Me and the people of Israel."

When God had finished talking to Moses on Mount Sinai, He gave Moses the two stone tablets of the covenant, on which God had inscribed the law with His own hand.

COMMENTARIES

From the Midrash

When God created the Sabbath, it complained that everything else that had been created had a partner. Only the Sabbath did not have a partner.

"Do not worry," said God. "You too will have a partner. The entire nation of Israel will be your partner. Throughout the ages Israel will watch over you and love you."

From Rashi

The Sabbath is not only a sign between God and Israel, but it is a sign between God and the whole world.

XX

The Golden Calf and Renewal

Exodus 32:1–40:38

The Israelites waiting at the foot of Mount Sinai become impatient because Moses has not returned. They ask Aaron to construct a golden calf for them to worship, and he does.

Moses comes down from the mountain, sees the people worshipping the golden calf, and is so angry that he smashes the tablets.

God also is angry but soon forgives them and inscribes another set of tablets, and a new covenant is established.

The Tabernacle is constructed according to specifications. A cloud covers it, and God's presence fills the Tabernacle.

Summary: EXODUS 32:1–29

When the people saw that Moses was so long in coming down from the mountain, they approached Aaron and said, "Make us a god who will lead us. We do not know what has happened to Moses, who led us out of Egypt."

Aaron said, "Take off your gold earrings and bring them to me." The people brought their gold earrings to Aaron, and Aaron melted them down and made a golden calf. Then he built an altar before it, and the people worshipped it and brought sacrifices to it.

God said to Moses,	וַיְדַבֵּר יְהֹוָה אֶת מֹשֶׁה
"Hurry down,	לֶךְ־רֵד
Because your people whom	כִּי שִׁחֵת עַמְּךָ אֲשֶׁר הֶעֱלֵיתָ מֵאֶרֶץ
you have saved from Egypt	מִצְרָיִם:
have gone astray."	

Moses pleaded for the people, and God renounced the punishment He had planned to bring on them.

Then Moses took the two tablets that had been inscribed by God and descended the mountain. As soon as he came near the camp and saw the calf, he was furious. He took the tablets that were in his hands and shattered them at the foot of the mountain. Then he took the calf that the people had made and burned it. He ground the cinders into a powder which he sprinkled on the water. Then he forced the Israelites to drink the water.

COMMENTARIES

From the Midrash

All the evil and all the suffering that the Children of Israel have endured are a result of their turning aside from God and constructing and worshipping the golden calf.

Moses smashed the tablets when he saw the golden calf out of love for the people of Israel. He knew that as long as they did not have the commandments and did not know the Torah, they would not be punished as severely for their sin.

SOMETHING TO THINK ABOUT

According to this Midrash the people could not be held accountable for disobeying the Torah because they had not yet received the Torah and so did not know that they were doing wrong. Do you think that the people were unaware that they were doing something wrong? Why do you think so? Is ignorance of the law an excuse for doing the wrong thing?

The next day Moses said to the people, "You have been guilty of a great sin. But I will go up to the Lord. Perhaps I may win forgiveness for you."

Moses pleaded with God, and God agreed, for Moses' sake, to forgive the Israelites and give Moses another set of tablets. So Moses carved two tablets of stone just like the first, and went up to Mount Sinai taking the tablets with him. There the Lord again established a covenant with the Children of Israel.

Moses was with the Lord for forty days and forty nights.

He ate no bread	לֶחֶם לֹא אָכַל
and drank no water;	וּמַיִם לֹא שָׁתָה
and he wrote down on the tab-lets the terms of the coven-ant,	וַיִּכְתֹּב עַל־הַלֻּחֹת אֵת דִּבְרֵי הַבְּרִית
the Ten Commandments.	עֲשֶׂרֶת הַדְּבָרִים:

Then Moses, his face radiant, came down from the mountain carrying the two tablets of the covenant. He instructed the Israelites concerning all that God had told him on Mount Sinai.

COMMENTARIES

From the Midrash

Before God gave the Torah to the Israelites he offered it to various other nations of the world. "Will you accept and obey My Torah?" He asked the first nation.

"What does it say?" they asked.

"It says 'You shall not kill,' answered God.

"We cannot accept and obey the Torah," answered the first nation. "Throughout our history we have lived by the sword."

Then God asked the second nation, "Will you accept and obey My Torah?"

"What does it say?" they asked.

"It says 'Honor your father and your mother,' " answered God.

"We cannot accept and obey the Torah," answered the second nation. "We reject our parents when they grow old."

God asked all the nations of the world. But none would promise to accept and obey the Torah. Then He asked Israel. The Israelites did not ask what was in the Torah. They did not hesitate. They answered, "All that God has spoken we will do and we will obey."

Moses gathered the entire community of the Children of Israel and said to them, "These are the things that the Lord has commanded you to do:

On six days work may be done,	שֵׁשֶׁת יָמִים תֵּעָשֶׂה מְלָאכָה
but on the seventh day you shall have a Sabbath of complete rest,	וּבַיּוֹם הַשְּׁבִיעִי יִהְיֶה לָכֶם קֹדֶשׁ שַׁבַּת שַׁבָּתוֹן
holy to the Lord.	לַיהוָֹה .

You shall kindle no fire on the seventh day throughout your settlements."

Then Moses told the Israelites that God had commanded them to build a Tabernacle for the Ten Commandments. Everyone who excelled in ability and talent, and everyone whose spirit moved him, was to come and bring with him his offering for building the Tabernacle. They brought their jewelry and gold objects of all kinds. They brought blue, purple, and crimson yarn, fine linen, goat's hair, tanned ram skins, and dolphin skins. They brought gifts of silver and copper and acacia wood. All the men and women whose hearts moved them to bring anything for the work that the Lord had commanded brought it as a free-will offering to the Lord. Bezalel, who was divinely endowed with skill and knowledge of every kind of craft, made the designs and directed the work.

COMMENTARIES

From the Midrash

Contributing gold and precious gifts for the Tabernacle was the way that the Children of Israel atoned for their sin in having worshipped the golden calf. By accepting the gifts and allowing the Tabernacle to be built, God showed the Israelites and the entire world that He had forgiven them for the sin of the golden calf.

From Nachmanides

The Exodus from Egypt was not complete until the Tabernacle had been built and the presence of God was in it in the midst of the Israelites.

When the Tabernacle was completed as God had commanded, the Israelites brought it to Moses. Moses saw that they had performed all the tasks.

As the Lord had commanded,	כַּאֲשֶׁר צִוָּה יְהוָֹה
so they had done.	כֵּן עָשׂוּ
And Moses blessed them.	וַיְבָרֶךְ אֹתָם מֹשֶׁה:

In the first month of the second year, on the first of the month, Moses set up the Tabernacle. He spread the tent over it, as God had commanded, and placed the tablets of the covenant in the ark. Then he screened off the ark and set up everything else as the Lord had commanded.

When Moses had finished the work, a cloud covered the Tent of Meeting and the presence of the Lord filled the Tabernacle. A cloud of the Lord rested by day over the Tabernacle and fire appeared in it at night, in the view of all the house of Israel throughout their journeys.

COMMENTARIES

From the Midrash

When God asked Moses to tell the Children of Israel to build a sanctuary for Him, Moses was surprised. "Even heaven and earth cannot contain you," said Moses. "How can You be contained in a sanctuary which we will build for you?"

God answered, "I do not need your sanctuary for My sake. It is for the people's sake that you must build it.

XXI

Laws and Rituals

Leviticus 1:1–18:30

Moses is called by God and told to relate to the Children of Israel the laws and rituals by which they are to live.

Laws and rituals in various categories are enumerated, including laws of sacrifice, dietary laws, laws and rituals relating to Yom Kippur, and laws of purity.

Summary: LEVITICUS 1:1–7:38

The Lord called to Moses from the Tent of Meeting and told him to speak to the Children of Israel and tell them the following regarding sacrifices:

When a burnt-offering is sacrificed to the Lord it shall be a male animal from the herd without blemish. The sons of Aaron the priest are to offer it up by placing it on the altar and burning it with fire, so that it is entirely consumed by the flame.

When a person presents an offering of meal to the Lord, his offering shall be of choice flour. He shall pour oil and frankincense on it and present it to Aaron' sons, the priests, who will burn it on the altar as an offering to God.

If a person offers a sacrifice of well-being, he shall bring a male or female animal without blemish from his herd. Only specified portions shall be offered on the altar. The rest shall be a festive meal for the sacrificer and his guests.

If a person without meaning to, commits a sin, he shall offer a sin-offering to the Lord. He shall sacrifice to the Lord an animal without blemish. Specified portions shall be burnt, and the remainder shall be eaten by the priests. The priests shall sacrifice in his behalf for the sin of which he is guilty, and he shall be forgiven.

When a person sins against the Lord by misappropriating property from another person or defrauding another person, he must restore that which he got through robbery or fraud and add a fifth to it. He shall pay it to the owner when he realizes his guilt. Then he shall bring a guilt-offering to the priest, who will sacrifice it to the Lord in his behalf, and he shall be forgiven.

COMMENTARIES

From the Midrash

When offering a sacrifice to God, it is not important whether one offers a little or a great deal. What is important is that whatever is offered is offered with a full heart and that the offerer's thoughts and feelings are directed to God.

Then Moses ordained Aaron and his sons into the priesthood. Moses assembled the people at the Tent of Meeting. Then, as God had commanded, he brought Aaron and his sons forward and washed them with water. He dressed them in vestments, as God had commanded. He anointed Aaron's head with oil and anointed the Tabernacle and all that was in it, thus making them holy. Moses then prepared a sin-offering which Aaron and his sons offered to God.

When this had all been done according to God's command,

God spoke to Aaron, saying,	וַיְדַבֵּר יְהֹוָה אֶל־אַהֲרֹן לֵאמֹר:
"Drink no wine or other intoxicating drink,	יַיִן וְשֵׁכָר אַל תֵּשְׁתְּ
you or your sons with you,	אַתָּה וּבָנֶיךָ אִתָּךְ
when you enter the Tent of Meeting,	בְּבֹאֲכֶם אֶל־אֹהֶל מוֹעֵד
that you may not die.	וְלֹא תָמֻתוּ
It is a law for all time throughout the ages.	חֻקַּת עוֹלָם לְדֹרֹתֵיכֶם:

For you must distinguish between the holy and the everyday, and between the clean and the unclean. And you must teach to the Children of Israel all the laws which the Lord gave to Moses."

COMMENTARIES

From the Talmud

The prohibition against drinking intoxicating liquor applies not only to priests. All who are teachers of Torah must refrain from drinking alcohol while teaching. If a teacher is asked a question when he has been drinking wine, he may not answer the question until the effects of the wine have worn off.

The Lord spoke to Moses and Aaron, saying, "Speak to the Israelite people and tell them that they may eat from among all the land animals only those that have cleft hooves and chew their cud. But those that do not both have cleft hooves and chew their cud, such as the camel, the rabbit, and the pig, they may not eat.

"Of the animals that swim in the water they may eat all those that have fins and scales. But those that do not have fins or scales they may not eat.

"They may not eat the following birds: the eagle, the vulture, the falcon, the raven, the ostrich, the owl, the hawk, the stork, and the pelican.

"They may eat locusts of many varieties and grasshoppers. But they may not eat any other winged swarming thing."

The Lord spoke to Moses, saying, "This shall be a law for all time. On the tenth day of the seventh month you shall make atonement for all your sins. You shall practice self-denial and do no manner of work.

"It shall be a Sabbath of complete rest for you.

שַׁבַּת שַׁבָּתוֹן הִיא לָכֶם :

"It shall be a law for all time for the Israelites to make atonement once a year for all their sins."

COMMENTARIES

From the Mishnah

Yom Kippur is a day of self-denial. The following activities are some of those forbidden: eating, drinking, washing, sports, attending school, etc.

A person whose health would seriously be endangered by fasting on Yom Kippur is permitted to eat.

From the Midrash

On Yom Kippur God forgives only those sins that are committed against God. Sins committed against another person can only be forgiven by the person who was wronged.

143

LEARNING MORE ABOUT:
THE TORAH SCROLL

When the Torah is read in the synagogue it is read from a parchment scroll. (This is the way books were written in ancient times.) Each Torah scroll is made up of many sheets of parchment (specially prepared animal skins). The sheets are sewn together with special sinews and attached to two wooden rollers.

The words of the Torah are handwritten on the parchment with a feather pen, or quill. The words are written without vowels, and the sentences do not have any punctuation. The number of paragraphs on each sheet of the scroll and the arrangement of the lines is always the same, so that a Torah read in your synagogue is exactly the same, line for line, as a Torah read in a synagogue many thousands of miles away.

A Torah scroll is written by a specially trained scholar called a scribe (sofer). Writing a Torah scroll is not just a difficult task, it is a religious responsibility, and the scribe is constantly aware of the sacred work he is doing.

A scribe *(sofer)* with a Torah scroll.

XXII
The Holiness Code

Leviticus 19:1–27:34

God commands the Israelites to observe special laws and commandments, for they are a holy people. These include moral and ethical practices as well as religious rituals.

Summary: LEVITICUS 19:1–37

The Lord spoke to Moses, saying, "Speak to the whole Israelite community and say to them,

'You shall be holy,
for I, the Lord your God, am holy.

קְדֹשִׁים תִּהְיוּ
כִּי קָדוֹשׁ אֲנִי יְהוָה אֱלֹהֵיכֶם:

'Fear your father and mother, and keep My Sabbaths.
'Do not turn to idols.
'When you sacrifice an offering of well-being to the Lord, it shall be eaten on the day it is offered or the day after. After that, what is left may not be eaten but must be burned.
'When you reap your harvest, do not gather from the edges of your field. When you gather the fruits of your vineyard, do not pick them bare or pick up what is fallen. You shall leave them for the poor and the strangers.
'You shall not steal.
'You shall not deal deceitfully or falsely with one another.
'You shall not swear falsely.
'You shall not cheat your neighbor.
'You shall not commit robbery.

'The wages of a hired man shall not remain with you until morning.

'You shall not insult the deaf or place a stumbling block before the blind.

'You shall judge your neighbors fairly. Do not favor the poor or show partiality to the rich.

'You shall not hate your brother in your heart. But you shall love your neighbor as yourself.

'You shall observe My laws.

'You shall not plant your fields with two different kinds of seed.

'You shall not wear cloth made of different materials.

'When you plant a tree for food, you may not eat of its fruit for three years. In the fourth year set aside the fruit for the Lord. You may eat of the fruit only in the fifth year.

'You shall not eat anything with its blood.

'You shall show respect for the aged.

'You shall treat a stranger in your community as one of your citizens, for you were strangers in the land of Egypt.

'You shall not falsify measures of length, weight, or capacity. But you shall have honest scales and measuring instruments.

'I am the Lord your God, who brought you out of the land of Egypt. You shall faithfully observe all My laws and all My rules. I am the Lord.'"

COMMENTARIES

From the Talmud

Hillel was a great scholar and a wise teacher. He was also known as a kindly and patient man who never lost his temper. One day a young man tried to see how far Hillel could be provoked before he would lose his temper. He went to him and asked him many silly questions. But Hillel did not lose his temper. He answered each question patiently. Finally, the young man thought of a question that he was sure would provoke Hillel to anger. He asked, "Hillel, can you teach me the whole Torah while I stand on one foot?"

Hillel did not get angry. Instead he thought for a moment. Then he answered, "You shall not hate your brother in your heart. But you shall love your neighbor as yourself. That is the whole Torah. The rest is merely commentary."

The young man was so impressed with the answer that he became a student of Hillel and studied Torah for the rest of his life.

"You shall love your neighbor as yourself." Rabbi Akiba said, "This is a fundamental principle of the Torah."

From the Midrash

The commandment "Do not place a stumbling block before the blind" has another meaning in addition to the obvious one. It means that one person may not act in such a way as to trick another into violating the Torah.

From Rashi

"Do not put a stumbling block before the blind" is meant not only in the physical sense. The implication is, "Do not give wrong advice to a person who is 'blind' in a particular matter—that is, he does not know the facts."

God said to Moses, "Speak to the Children of Israel and tell them that these are my fixed times which are sacred occasions:

The Sabbath: For six days work may be done, but on the seventh day you shall do no work; it shall be a Sabbath to the Lord your God.

Passover: On the fourteenth day of the first month at twilight, there shall be a Passover offering to the Lord. Beginning on the fifteenth day, for seven days you shall eat unleavened bread. You shall not work on the first day and on the seventh day, which shall be sacred occasions.

The Omer Period: When you enter the land I am giving you and reap its harvest, bring your first sheaf of wheat of the harvest to the priest. He shall wave it before the Lord for acceptance on the day after the Sabbath. From the day the sheaf is offered, you shall count off seven weeks.

Shavuoth: On the fiftieth day you shall bring an offering of new grain to the Lord. You shall also bring animal sacrifices and the bread of first fruits. On that same day you shall hold a celebration—it shall be a sacred occasion for you. You shall not work at your occupation. This is a law for all times throughout the ages.

Rosh Hashana: On the first day of the seventh month you shall observe complete rest, a sacred occasion commemorated with loud blasts on the shofar. You shall not work at your occupation, and you shall bring an offering by fire to the Lord.

Yom Kippur: On the tenth day of the seventh month is the Day of Atonement. It shall be a sacred occasion for you. You shall practice self-denial, and you shall bring an offering by fire to the Lord. You shall do no work throughout the day, for it is a day of atonement. It shall be a Sabbath of complete rest for you from evening to evening.

Succoth: On the fifteenth day of the seventh month there shall be the Feast of Booths to last seven days. The first and last days shall be sacred occasions on which you shall not work. You shall live in booths seven days, so that future generations may know that I made the Israelites live in booths when I brought them out of the land of Egypt. On the eighth day you shall observe a sacred occasion and bring an offering to the Lord. It is a solemn gathering."

Moses did as God had commanded and declared to the Israelites the set times of God.

COMMENTARIES

From the Midrash

Rabbi Joshua ben Chananiah and Emperor Antoninus of Rome were friends. One day the emperor was invited to share the Shabbat meal at the home of Rabbi Joshua. Everything was so delicious that the emperor asked for the recipes for the food he had eaten so that it could be prepared for him by his own cook. When the emperor's cook prepared the same food he had eaten at Rabbi Joshua's Sabbath meal and served it to him in the palace, the emperor found that it did not taste as good as in Rabbi Joshua's humble surroundings.

"How can it be that my cook prepared the same food in the same way and yet it tasted better in your home?" the emperor asked his friend.

"It is very simple," answered the rabbi. "The food you ate at my home was eaten on Shabbat. The Sabbath has its own special flavor that cannot be copied."

The Lord spoke to Moses and said, "When you enter the land that I give you, you shall observe a Sabbath of the land, a Sabbatical year. For six years you may plant your fields and gather the harvest. But in the seventh year you shall not plant your field. It shall be a year of complete rest for the land.

"In the fiftieth year you shall observe a Jubilee year. You shall count off forty-nine years. In the fiftieth year, on the Day of Atonement, the shofar shall be sounded throughout the land. You shall make the fiftieth year holy.

Proclaim liberty throughout the land	וּקְרָאתֶם דְּרוֹר בָּאָרֶץ
to all the inhabitants thereof.	לְכָל יֹשְׁבֶיהָ .

"In this year of Jubilee each of you shall return to his holding. When you sell or buy property you shall not wrong one another, but fear your God, for I am the Lord your God. Do not sell the land forever, for the land is Mine. You are but strangers and settlers with Me.

"If your brother becomes poor and must sell himself to you, do not make him serve as a slave. He shall be a hired servant and serve you only until the Jubilee year. Then you shall release him and his children from your service, and he shall return to his own family and property. For the Israelites are My servants. I brought them out of Egypt, and they shall not be sold as slaves. Do not rule over them harshly, but fear your God."

COMMENTARIES

From the Talmud

The law of the Jubilee year was observed as long as the entire territory of the Holy Land was inhabited by Israelites. When a portion of the Children of Israel went into exile, the laws of the Jubilee year no longer applied.

From Maimonides

Although the Torah only mentions that the Israelite slave is to be treated with kindness, we are to understand from this that all slaves, Jewish or Gentile, are to be treated by their Jewish owners with kindness.

God said to the Children of Israel, "If you follow My laws and faithfully observe My commandments I will grant you rains in their season, so that the earth wil yield its produce and the trees their fruit.

"I will grant peace in the land, and you shall go to sleep untroubled by anyone.

"I will favor you, and you will be fertile and multiply. And I will keep My covenant with you, and you shall be My people.

"But if you do not obey Me and observe these commandments, I will punish you seven times over for your sins. Your land shall not yield produce, and your trees shall not yield fruit.

"But when at last you atone for your sins, I will remember My covenant with Jacob and with Isaac and with Abraham, and I will remember My covenant with your ancestors whom I freed from the land of Egypt to be their God. I am the Lord."

COMMENTARIES

From Rashi

God promises to remember His covenant with Jacob, Isaac, and Abraham. The reason the patriarchs are mentioned in reverse order is to show that Jacob himself did enough good deeds so that for his sake alone all the Israelites may be redeemed. But if Jacob's deeds are not enough, then God will also consider the good deeds of Isaac. And if the good deeds of Jacob and Isaac are not enough, then God will also remember the good deeds of Abraham.

FOCUS ON:
BIBLICAL SELECTIONS IN THE PRAYERBOOK

The following passage from Leviticus 26 is in the Morning Service (Shacharit).

I will remember My covenant with Jacob	וְזָכַרְתִּי אֶת בְּרִיתִי יַעֲקוֹב,
and My covenant with Isaac,	וְאַף אֶת בְּרִיתִי יִצְחָק,
and I will remember My covenant with Abraham,	וְאַף־אֶת־בְּרִיתִי אַבְרָהָם אֶזְכֹּר,
and I will remember the land.	וְהָאָרֶץ אֶזְכֹּר.

LEARNING MORE ABOUT:
LAND IN ISRAEL

Every fifty years the Israelites observed a Jubilee year. The year was announced by the blowing of the shofar on Yom Kippur.

Special rules were observed during the Jubilee year. The land was not to be planted during that year; Hebrew slaves were given their liberty; and all land which had been sold went back to its original owner. This was because the land was considered God's property, which cannot be owned. It can only be *used* by those who have possession of it.

The idea that the land is God's property and can only be *used* by those who have it was very important in the development of modern Israel. It was the basis of the philosophy of the Jewish National Fund, an organization formed in 1901. The Jewish National Fund (JNF) collected money from Jews all over the world. The money was used to buy land in Israel that belonged to the entire Jewish people. The land was made available to Jews who wished to settle in Israel. They could live there and cultivate the land. But they could not sell it. As long as they took good care of it, the land remained with them. But they had an obligation to manage the land properly so as to conserve natural resources.

Most of the land in Israel at the present time is the property of the Jewish National Fund. It can neither be bought nor sold. It can only be rented for long periods of time. In this way the Jews of Israel follow the spirit of the law that the land belongs to God and people cannot own it.

FOCUS ON:
THE LIBERTY BELL

The Liberty Bell, which is an important symbol of American democracy, has engraved on it a verse from the Bible. The verse is Leviticus 25:10 and it says, "Proclaim liberty throughout the land to all the inhabitants thereof." This was the phrase used in the Bible to proclaim the Jubilee year.

The Liberty Bell is located in Philadelphia, Pennsylvania. It was in Philadelphia, in 1776, that the Declaration of Independence was signed. After it was signed, the bell was rung to announce to the new nation that "liberty" had been "proclaimed throughout the land."

The Liberty Bell remains, to this day, a national historic treasure. Many visitors from other countries, as well as Americans, visit Independence Hall every year to see the Liberty Bell and read the inscription from the Bible.

The Liberty Bell in Philadelphia. The inscription on the bell is from the third book of the Bible, Leviticus XXV:10, reading "Proclaim liberty throughout the land, unto all the inhabitants thereof."

XXIII

The Wilderness of Sinai

Numbers 1:1−10:10

Moses is commanded to take a census of the Israelite community in which every male over the age of twenty who is able to bear arms is listed. The priestly families are separately counted and their duties are enumerated.

The Israelites continue their travels in the desert, guided by a cloud, which is God's sign, over the Tabernacle. The visual sign of the cloud is supplemented by the blowing of silver trumpets by the priests.

Summary: NUMBERS 1:1−2:34

In the second year following the Exodus from Egypt, the Lord spoke to Moses in the wilderness of Sinai from the Tent of Meeting, saying, "Take a census of the entire Israelite community, according to the families, and list the name of every male from the age of twenty up—all those in Israel who are able to bear arms."

Moses and Aaron, assisted by the chiefs of the tribes, gathered the whole community and recorded the names of those aged twenty years and over according to their ancestral families. All those in Israel who were able to bear arms were enrolled. In all, those who were registered came to 603,550.

The Levites were not recorded according to their ancestral families. God said, "Do not enroll the tribes of Levi. Put them in charge of the Tabernacle and all its furnishings. They shall tend the Tabernacle and camp around it. They shall stand guard around the Tabernacle."

Then God said, "The Israelites shall camp according to their ancestral families, each with its own flag, around the Tent of Meeting at a distance."

The Israelites did just as the Lord commanded Moses. They camped by their banners, and when they marched, they marched each with his clan according to his ancestral family.

COMMENTARIES

From the Midrash

Each tribe had a flag of a different color. The colors corresponded to the colors of the precious stones on Aaron's breastplate. It was from these flags that governments learned to provide themselves with flags of various colors.

When the tribes camped around the Tabernacle, they did not have to be told where to position themselves. They positioned themselves in the same way that their ancestors, the sons of Jacob, had positioned themselves around the casket of Jacob at his funeral.

The Lord spoke to Moses, saying, "Assign the tribe of Levi to Aaron the priest to serve him. They shall perform duties for him and for the whole community before the Tent of Meeting, doing the work of the Tabernacle and being in charge of its furnishings.

"Make Aaron and his sons responsible for observing the priestly duties. Speak to them and say: 'Thus shall you bless the people of Israel:

The Lord bless you and keep you!	יְבָרֶכְךָ יהוָה וְיִשְׁמְרֶךָ:
The Lord cause His face to shine upon you and be gracious to you!	יָאֵר יהוָה ׀ פָּנָיו אֵלֶיךָ וִיחֻנֶּךָּ:
The Lord lift up His face to you and grant you peace!	יִשָּׂא יהוָה ׀ פָּנָיו אֵלֶיךָ וְיָשֵׂם לְךָ שָׁלוֹם:

COMMENTARIES

From the Midrash

The Children of Israel complained to God, "You tell the priests to bless us. But we want only Your blessing."

God answered, "Although I have told the priests to bless you, I will be right there in their company when they carry out the blessing."

From Bachya

In the priestly benediction the first blessing has three words (in the Hebrew), the second blessing has five words, and the third blessing has seven words. This reminds us that the three patriarchs, the five books of the Torah, and the seven heavens are the basis of all blessings.

From the day that the Tabernacle was set up it was covered by a cloud by day. At night, it was covered by a fire until morning. When the cloud lifted from the Tent, the Israelites would set out on their journey. When the cloud settled again over the Tabernacle, they would make camp. On a sign from the Lord, the Israelites broke camp and proceeded on their journey, and on a sign from the Lord, they made camp. They encamped as long as the cloud stayed over the Tabernacle, even if it remained there for many days or many months.

Then the Lord spoke to Moses and said, "Have two silver trumpets made. They shall serve to summon the community. Aaron's sons, the priests, shall blow them. When you are in your own land and you are at war against an aggressor who attacks you, sound short blasts on the trumpets and I will deliver you from your enemies. Sound your trumpets also on joyous occasions, on festivals and new moons, or when you bring your sacrifices. They shall be a reminder of you before the Lord your God."

COMMENTARIES

From the Midrash

When the Tabernacle was set up the world became firmly established. Before that it had been unstable.

XXIV

Rebellions and Victories

The people become dissatisfied and complain. God provides additional food, but in His anger He strikes the people with a plague.

Moses sends scouts to explore the promised land. They return with both good and bad reports of conditions there.

Korah, Dathan, and Abiram rebel against Moses, but their action ends in failure and they are destroyed.

Time passes. Miriam dies. Moses, again faced by a rebellious people, reacts in anger and is told that as a result he will not enter the promised land. Aaron dies. There are various battles with Canaanites, Amorites, and others in which the Israelites, aided by God, are victorious.

Summary: NUMBERS 10:11–12:16

On the twentieth day of the second month in the second year, the cloud lifted from the Tabernacle and the Israelites set out on their journey from the wilderness of Sinai.

They marched from the Mountain of the Lord a distance of three days. The Ark of the Covenant of the Lord traveled in front of them. And the Lord's cloud kept above them by day as they moved on from camp.

But the people took to complaining bitterly against God. They wept and said, "If only we had meat to eat. We remember the fish we used to eat free in Egypt—the cucumbers, the melons, the leeks, the onions, and the garlic. Now we have nothing to eat but manna."

Moses heard the people crying. He was very upset and said to the Lord, "Are you not pleased with me? Why have you placed the burden of this people on me? Why have you made me responsible for them? Where am I to get meat to give them?"

The Lord said to Moses, "Say to the people: Be ready, for tomorrow we shall eat meat. The Lord will give you meat and you shall eat."

The next day a wind from the sea blew in quail from the sea and scattered them on the ground all over the camp. The people gathered quail all that day and the next night. But still there were more, and they ate their fill. But the meat was still between their teeth, not yet chewed, when God's anger flared up against the people, and they were struck by a terrible plague.

COMMENTARIES

From Rashi

It was not true that the Israelites did not have meat to eat. We are told in other parts of the text that they had flocks of birds and herds of cattle. The truth was that the rebels were just looking for an excuse to complain.

How could the Children of Israel say that in Egypt they were given fish and other delicacies free when the Egyptians did not even provide them with straw to make their quotas of bricks? By "free" they meant without obligation to God. Moses made God's bounty dependent on loyalty to God's laws. But in Egypt the people were free of such obligations.

FOCUS ON:
BIBLICAL SELECTIONS IN THE PRAYERBOOK

The following passages from Numbers 10 are included in the Morning
Torah Service.

When the ark was to set out,	וַיְהִי בִּנְסֹעַ הָאָרֹן
Moses would say:	וַיֹּאמֶר מֹשֶׁה.
"Go forward, O God!	קוּמָה יְהֹוָה וְיָפֻצוּ אֹיְבֶיךָ,
May your enemies flee before you."	וְיָנֻסוּ מְשַׂנְאֶיךָ מִפָּנֶיךָ.
And when it stopped, he would say:	וּבְנֻחֹה יֹאמַר:
"Return, O God.	שׁוּבָה יְהֹוָה
to the multitudes of the families of Israel.	רִבְבוֹת אַלְפֵי יִשְׂרָאֵל:

The Lord spoke to Moses, saying, "Send men to scout the land of Canaan which I am giving to the Israelite people."

So Moses did as God commanded and sent out men who were leaders of the Israelites.

And Moses said to them,

	וַיֹּאמֶר אֲלֵהֶם
"Go up there into the Negev	עֲלוּ זֶה בַּנֶּגֶב
and on into the hill country,	וַעֲלִיתֶם אֶת־הָהָר:
and see what kind of country it is.	וּרְאִיתֶם אֶת־הָאָרֶץ מַה־הִוא
Are the people who live there strong or weak—few or many?	וְאֶת־הָעָם הַיֹּשֵׁב עָלֶיהָ הֶחָזָק הוּא הֲרָפֶה הַמְעַט הוּא אִם־רָב.

Is the country where they live good or bad? Are the towns open or fortified? Is the soil rich or poor? Is it wooded or not? And remember to bring back with you samples of the fruit of the land."

The scouts left and scouted the land. They went to the wilderness of Zin and into the Negev. They went to Hebron and Eshcol. In Eshcol they cut down a branch with a single cluster of grapes. It was so heavy that it took two men to carry it. They also brought back pomegranates and figs.

At the end of forty days they returned from scouting the land. They reported to Moses and Aaron and the whole community that they had found a land flowing with milk and honey. But they also reported that the people were powerful and that the cities were large and fortified. They said, "We cannot attack the people, for they are stronger than we."

The whole community broke into loud cries and wept all that night. The people said, "Let us go back to Egypt. If we stay and fight we shall die by the sword."

God was angry. He said to Moses, "Tell the Children of Israel that they shall not enter this land. They shall wander the desert for forty years until all in that generation are dead. Only their children shall enter the promised land."

COMMENTARIES

From the Midrash

Moses told the spies how they could tell if the Canaanites were strong or weak: "If the people live in fortified cities, they are afraid of being attacked, and you will know that they are weak. But if they live openly without fortifications, you will know that they are not afraid of being attacked because they are strong."

When Moses sent out the spies he sent them first to the Negev, the poorest part of the land. This is like a salesman who shows the least desirable merchandise first and only afterward brings out his more valuable wares.

Now Korah, Dathan, and Abiram rose up against Moses and Aaron and led a rebellion against them. They said, "You have gone too far. We are all holy, and the Lord is in our midst. Why then do you raise yourself above the Lord's congregation?"

When Moses heard this, he fell on his face and said, "You have gone too far. In the morning the Lord will make known to you who is His and who is holy."

Then the presence of God was felt in the whole community, and God spoke to Moses and Aaron, saying, "Stand back that I may destroy this community in an instant!"

But Moses and Aaron fell to the ground and said, "O God, source of all life, when one man sins will You be angry with the whole community?"

So God said to Moses,	וַיְדַבֵּר יְהֹוָה אֶל־מֹשֶׁה לֵּאמֹר:
"Speak to the community	דַּבֵּר אֶל־הָעֵדָה לֵאמֹר
and tell them to move away from the homes of Korah, Dathan, and Abiram."	הֵעָלוּ מִסָּבִיב לְמִשְׁכַּן־קֹרַח דָּתָן וַאֲבִירָם.

Then God made the earth to open up, and the rebels and their families were swallowed up whole, along with their possessions and their households. All Israel around them fled at their shrieks, for they were afraid that the earth might open and swallow them too.

COMMENTARIES

From the Midrash

When Korah, Dathan, and Abiram sinned, only they and their families were punished by God. This is unlike an earthly king, who often punishes all the people in a province if only one person rebels against him.

From Rashi

When Korah, Dathan, and Abiram and their households were swallowed up by the earth, their children were also swallowed up, although they were not responsible for the sins of their fathers. Although an earthly court does not punish children, the Heavenly Court makes even young children pay for the sins of their parents.

On the first new moon the Israelites arrived at the Wilderness of Zin. There Miriam died and was buried.

The community was without water, and all joined together against Moses and Aaron. "If only we had died when our brothers died," they said. "Why did you make us leave Egypt to bring us to this terrible place without grain or figs or vines or pomegranates? There is not even water to drink."

Moses and Aaron fell on their faces before God, and the Lord spoke to Moses, saying, "You and your brother Aaron, take your rod and gather the community about you. Before their eyes order the rock to yield its water!"

Moses gathered the Israelites about him. Then he raised his hand and struck the rock twice with his rod. Water flowed from the rock, and the people and their animals drank.

But the Lord said to Moses and Aaron, "Because you did not trust Me enough to do as I said, you shall not lead this congregation into the land that I have given them."

The Israelites continued on their journey through the wilderness. At Mount Hor, on the boundary of the land of Edom, God said to Moses and Aaron, "Let Aaron be gathered to his ancestors. He is not to enter the land that I have given to the Israelite people because you disobeyed My command about the Waters of Meribah." And so Aaron died and was mourned by all the household of Israel for thirty days.

After Aaron's death the Israelites continued on their journey. With the help of God they were victorious over the Canaanite king of Arad, Sihon, king of the Amorites, and Og, king of Bashan.

COMMENTARIES

From Maimonides

The reason that Moses was punished so severely for striking the rock was that the act of striking the rock was a display of temper. One who seeks to lead must not lose his temper in this manner.

LEARNING MORE ABOUT PLACES IN THE BIBLE: CANAAN

The promised land, called Canaan in the Bible, is the land we now call Israel. The boundaries of the Biblical land of Canaan extend from Dan in the north to below Beersheba in the south, and from the Mediterranean Sea in the west to the desert in the east. The total territory was about 10,000 square miles, the size of the State of New Hampshire.

The climate of Canaan (Israel) is very diverse. Mount Hermon in the north is very cold, while 100 miles to the south, in the Jordan Valley, Jericho has a hot, tropical climate. Jerusalem, on the other hand, enjoys a temperate climate. Israel has two seasons: a rainy season, which usually lasts from October through March; and a dry season for the rest of the year.

The climate of Isarel is excellent for agriculture, and both the ancient inhabitants of the land, like those who live there today, took advantage of the good farming conditions.

XXV
The Story of Balaam

Numbers 22:2–24:25

The Israelites continue their advance toward the promised land. Balak, the king of Moab, is concerned about the military might of the advancing Israelites. He hires Balaam to put a curse on the Israelites so that they can be defeated. But God intervenes on behalf of the Israelites. Instead of cursing them, Balaam blesses the Israelites and prophesies that all their enemies will be defeated.

Summary: NUMBERS 22:2–12

Balak son of Zippor, the king of Moab, saw all that Israel had done to the Amorites. Moab was alarmed because the Israelites were so numerous. So Balak sent princes as messengers to Balaam to say to him, "Come, put a curse on this people, since they are too numerous for me. For I know that he whom you bless is blessed indeed, and he whom you curse is cursed."

The messengers came to Balaam and gave him Balak's message. But God appeared to Balaam that night and said, "Do not go with them. You must not curse that people, for they are blessed."

COMMENTARIES

From the Midrash

Balaam was a true prophet, although he was a pagan. God gave the gift
of prophecy to men like Balaam so that the other nations might not say
that God loved only the Israelites.

From the Talmud

At first Balaam was a true prophet and spoke the words of God. But
then he deserted God and became a magician.

The next morning Balaam said to the messengers, "Go back to your own country, for the Lord will not let me go with you."

The messengers returned to their country. But Balak sent other messengers more important than the first. They offered Balaam silver and gold, but still Balaam refused to go.

That night God came to Balaam and said to him, "If these men have come to invite you, you may go with them. But whatever I command you, that you shall do."

When Balaam arose in the morning he saddled his donkey and left with the Moabite messengers. But an angel of God placed himself in Balaam's way. When the donkey saw the angel of God standing in the way with sword drawn, it swerved from the road and went into the fields. Balaam beat the donkey, and it returned to the road.

The angel of the Lord then positioned himself in a lane between two vineyards with a fence on either side. The donkey, seeing the angel, pressed itself against the wall and squeezed Balaam's foot against the wall. Again, Balaam beat the donkey. Then the angel positioned himself in a spot so narrow that there was no room to pass on either side. The donkey saw the angel in the way and lay down under Balaam. Balaam was so angry that he beat the donkey with a stick.

Then God opened the donkey's mouth and it said to Balaam, "What have I done to you that you have beaten me three times?"

Balaam said, "You have made me a laughing stock. If I had a sword, I would kill you."

The donkey said to Balaam, "Look, you have been riding me all this time. Have I ever done this before today?" And Balaam answered, "No."

Then Balaam looked up and saw the angel of the Lord. The angel said, "You beat the donkey. But it was I who stood in your way because I hate what you are doing."

Balaam answered, "If you still disapprove, I will turn back."

But the angel said, "Go with the men, but you must say nothing except what I tell you."

So Balaam went with Balak's messengers until they arrived at their destination.

COMMENTARIES

From the Midrash

At first Balaam was told not to go with the messengers. But when he insisted, God allowed him to go. From this we learn that God allows a person to do what his heart desires.

From Maimonides

There wasn't really a talking donkey. The incidents in the story happened only in Balaam's dream.

Balaam said to Balak, "Build for me seven altars, and prepare for me seven bulls and seven rams." Balak did as Balaam directed, and Balak and Balaam sacrificed a bull and a ram on each altar. Then Balaam said, "How can I curse whom God has not cursed?" And Balaam blessed the Children of Israel. Balaam saw that it pleased God when he blessed Israel. He looked up and saw the Israelites camped tribe by tribe, and the spirit of God came upon him and he continued to bless them, saying,

"How good are your tents,
  O Jacob,

מַה־טֹּבוּ אֹהָלֶיךָ יַעֲקֹב

"The places where you live,
  O Israel.

מִשְׁכְּנֹתֶיךָ יִשְׂרָאֵל:

> They are like palm groves that stretch out,
> Like gardens beside a river,
> Like cedars beside the water.
> God freed you from Egypt.
> Now you shall devour every nation.
> Blessed are those who bless you.
> And cursed are those who curse you."

Balak was furious with Balaam. He wrung his hands together and said, "I called you to curse my enemies and instead you bless them. Go back at once to your own place. I was going to reward you, but God has denied you the reward."

Balaam answered, "I even told the messengers you sent to me that I could not do anything good or bad against the Lord's command. What the Lord says, that I must say. This people will one day be triumphant over its enemies."

Then Balaam set out on his journey back home; and Balak also went on his way.

COMMENTARIES

From the Midrash

As soon as Balaam's donkey had finished speaking, it died. God did not want the people to say, "This is the animal that spoke," and make it an object of worship.

When Balaam looked up and saw the tents of the Israelites, he saw in his mind the schools of the Israelites where Torah would be taught. That is why he said, "How good are your tents, O Jacob."

XXVI

The Promised Land

Numbers 27:12–36:13

Moses is commanded to prepare for his death and choose Joshua as his successor.

The Israelites, led by Moses, engage in a war against the Midianites. After they are victorious they establish their first permanent settlement.

Six cities in Canaan are designated as "cities of refuge" where a person who has killed another without meaning to may escape from the vengeance of the victim's family and await trial.

Summary: NUMBERS 27:12–23

The Lord said to Moses, "Climb up on Mount Abarim and see the land that I have given to the Israelite people. When you have seen it, you shall be gathered to your ancestors, just as your brother Aaron was, because in the Wilderness of Zin you disobeyed Me regarding the water."

Moses spoke to God, saying, "Let the Lord appoint someone over the people to lead them, so that the Lord's community shall not be like sheep who have no shepherd."

The Lord answered, "Choose Joshua the son of Nun, who is an inspired man, and lay your hand upon him and commission him in the sight of the community.

"Give him some of your authority	וְנָתַתָּה מֵהוֹדְךָ עָלָיו
so that the whole Israelite community may obey him."	לְמַעַן יִשְׁמְעוּ כָּל־עֲדַת בְּנֵי יִשְׂרָאֵל׃

Moses did as the Lord commanded. He took Joshua and laid his hands upon him and commissioned him, as the Lord had said.

COMMENTARIES

From the Midrash

When Moses laid his hands on Joshua and commissioned him to be his successor, it was like one candle lighting another. The first candle continues to burn as brightly as before.

From Rashi

In the text we read that God told Moses to lay his "hand" on Joshua and commission him. But later we read that Moses laid his "hands" on Joshua and commissioned him. From this we learn that Moses was even more generous to Joshua than God had commanded. He bestowed his wisdom on him very generously.

Then the Lord spoke to Moses, saying, "Lead the Israelite people in getting revenge on the Midianites. After that you shall be gathered to your ancestors."

So Moses spoke to the people and told them to wage a military campaign against Midian. They did, and they were victorious. They killed every male, took the women and children captive, and carried away the wealth and the flocks as booty. Then they destroyed all the camps and towns by fire, and they brought the booty to Moses.

When all this had been done, the men of the tribes of Gad and Reuben came to Moses and said, "The land that the Lord has conquered for the community is cattle country, and we have cattle. It would be a favor to us if this land were given to us as our possession."

But Moses answered, "Shall your brothers continue to wage war while you remain here on this land?" And they said to him, "We will build cities here for our families, and they shall live here until we return. But we shall cross over to engage in battle until our brothers have secured their inheritance. Then we will return to our homes."

COMMENTARIES

From the Midrash

Moses did not want the men of the tribes of Gad and Reuben to remain behind in the conquered territory of Midian, because he was afraid that if he granted their request it would discourage the other tribes, since it would reduce the fighting strength of Israel.

The Lord spoke to Moses, saying, "Tell the people to set aside towns for the Levites to live in. You shall also assign to the Levites pasture land around the towns. The towns that you assign to the Levites shall include six cities of refuge which you are to set aside so that a person who kills another without meaning to can flee there. These cities shall be a refuge from the avengers so that the killer may not die until he has stood trial before the assembly. The cities of refuge shall be for the Israelites and also for the resident aliens among you.

"But anyone who kills another by striking him with an iron object is a murderer and must be put to death. So too, if he pushes him in hate or throws something at him on purpose and death results, or if he strikes him with his hand in hatred and death results, he is a murderer and shall be put to death.

"But if he pushes him without malice, or throws an object at him unintentionally, or accidentally drops a deadly object of stone on him and death results—though he was not an enemy of his, and he did not seek to hurt him—in such cases the assembly shall decide between the killer and the one who wants to kill him for revenge.

"Such shall be your law of procedure through the ages. If anyone kills another person he can be convicted only on the evidence of witnesses—the testimony of a single witness is not enough for a sentence of death."

COMMENTARIES

From the Midrash

If God is so concerned with the rights of the person who commits manslaughter, how much more concerned is He about the rights and well-being of the righteous.

LEARNING MORE ABOUT:
CITIES OF REFUGE

In Biblical times, if one person killed another, the victim's family was permitted to kill the killer in revenge. But this held true only if the killing was an intentional murder.

If one person killed another accidentally, he could escape to one of the cities of refuge that had been set aside for this purpose. The victim's family was not permitted to pursue the killer there. The killer stayed in the city of refuge until a trial was held to decide whether the killing was done on purpose or accidentally. If it was decided that the killing was accidental, the killer could remain in the city of refuge, where he continued to be safe from the avenger. But if it was decided that the victim was killed on purpose, then the killer would have to go back to the place where the crime took place and where he was at the mercy of the victim's family.

XXVII

The Covenant Between God and Israel

Deuteronomy 1:1−5:30

Moses speaks to the Children of Israel at the end of their forty years of wandering and reminds them of their history during the forty years in the wilderness. He then summarizes the elements of the covenant between God and Israel and what God requires of them. The Ten Commandments are repeated, and the Israelites are again warned to obey them.

Summary: DEUTERONOMY 1:1−3:29

These are the words that Moses spoke to all Israel on the other side of the Jordan. (It was in the fortieth year, on the first day of the eleventh month, that Moses addressed the Israelites, as the Lord had instructed him.)

"Make your way to the hill country of the Amorites and to all their neighbors in the lowlands, the Negev, the seacoast, the land of the Canaanites, and Lebanon as far as the River Euphrates. I place this land before you. Go and take possession of it. For the Lord swore to give it to your ancestors Abraham, Isaac, and Jacob, and to all their descendants after them.

"Together we set out from Horeb (Sinai) and traveled the great and terrible wilderness. When we came to the hill country of the Amorites, which the Lord our God is giving to us, you asked me to send men ahead to spy out the land. I selected twelve men and they spied it out. They brought some of the fruit of the land back to us and reported that it is a good land. Yet you refused to go, and you complained. You saw how the Lord took care of you in the wilderness, and yet for all that you had no faith in the Lord

179

your God, who leads you on your journeys in fire by night and as a cloud by day.

"The Lord was angry and swore that the evil generation would not see the good land. Because of them the Lord was angry at me too, and would not let me enter the land, but said that Joshua the son of Nun would enter it as your leader.

"We traveled (for thirty-eight years) until that whole generation had perished. I pleaded with the Lord at that time to let me cross over and see the land on the other side of the Jordan. But the Lord was angry with me and would not listen to me, and told me never to speak of this matter again, but to give Joshua his instructions and inspire him with strength and courage, for he would go across as your head and lead you to the land that only you may see."

COMMENTARIES

From the Midrash

When Moses was a young man, and God called to him from the burning bush and asked him to speak to Pharaoh on behalf of the Israelites, and ask Pharaoh to let the Israelites go, Moses was doubtful of his ability to make himself understood, because he was a "person slow of speech." But after receiving the Torah, Moses no longer hestitated to speak. He became confident and spoke of the Torah often and eloquently.

From Rashi

Moses spoke angrily and critically to the Israelites. He knew that a leader should praise more than criticize. But he knew that he was near death and that the words of criticism must be spoken before he died.

"And now, O Israel, pay attention to the laws and rules which I am instructing you to observe, so that you may live to enter the land that the Lord is giving you. What great nation has laws and rules as perfect as this teaching that I have set before you this day? The Lord our God made a covenant with us at Horeb (Sinai).

It was not only with our ancestors that the Lord made this covenant,	לֹא אֶת־אֲבֹתֵינוּ כָּרַת יְהוָֹה אֶת־הַבְּרִית הַזֹּאת
but with us the living,	כִּי אִתָּנוּ
every one of us who is here today.	אֲנַחְנוּ אֵלֶּה פֹה הַיּוֹם כֻּלָּנוּ חַיִּים׃

The Lord spoke to you face to face on the mountain, out of the fire. I stood between the Lord and you at that time to convey His words to you, for you were afraid of the fire and did not go up on the mountain. And the Lord spoke these words:

God spoke all these words saying:

'I am the Lord your God who brought you out of the land of Egypt, out of the house of bondage.

אָנֹכִי יְהֹוָה אֱלֹהֶיךָ אֲשֶׁר הוֹצֵאתִיךָ מֵאֶרֶץ מִצְרַיִם מִבֵּית עֲבָדִים:

'You shall have no other gods beside Me.

לֹא־יִהְיֶה לְךָ אֱלֹהִים אֲחֵרִים עַל־פָּנָי:

'You shall not take the name of the Lord in vain.

לֹא תִשָּׂא אֶת־שֵׁם־יְהֹוָה אֱלֹהֶיךָ לַשָּׁוְא

'Observe the Sabbath to keep it holy.

שָׁמוֹר אֶת־יוֹם הַשַּׁבָּת לְקַדְּשׁוֹ

'Honor your father and your mother.

כַּבֵּד אֶת־אָבִיךָ וְאֶת־אִמֶּךָ

'You shall not murder.

לֹא תִרְצָח:

'You shall not be unfaithful to wife or husband.

וְלֹא תִנְאָף:

'You shall not steal.

וְלֹא תִגְנֹב:

'You shall not bear false witness.

וְלֹא־תַעֲנֶה בְרֵעֲךָ עֵד שָׁוְא:

'You shall not desire what is your neighbor's.'

וְלֹא תַחְמֹד אֵשֶׁת רֵעֶךָ.

"The Lord spoke those words to your whole congregation at the mountain. He inscribed them on the tablets of stone which He gave me. Be careful then to do as the Lord your God commanded you. Follow only the path that the Lord has commanded you so that it may go well with you."

COMMENTARIES

From the Midrash

The words of the Torah can be compared to a bee. The bee's honey is sweet, but its sting is sharp. The words of the Torah are also sweet, but if one disobeys them, then the punishment is severe.

From Maimonides

God set the commandments before us, but we can decide whether or not to obey them. Every person has free will. He can be righteous or wicked. Since all the wicked deeds we commit are committed willfully, we can blame no one for them and must repent and make amends. This power is within our hands. It is the basis of the commandments and of all law.

FOCUS ON:
BIBLICAL SELECTIONS IN THE PRAYERBOOK

The following passage from Deuteronomy 4 is in the Torah Service.

You who hold fast to the Eternal,	וְאַתֶּם הַדְּבֵקִים בַּיהוָֹה אֱלֹהֵיכֶם,
your God, are all alive today.	חַיִּים כֻּלְּכֶם הַיּוֹם.

LEARNING MORE ABOUT BIBLICAL COMMENTARIES:
THE ZOHAR

The study of Jewish mysticism is known as the Kabbalah. One of the most important parts of the Kabbalah is a book of mysticism called the Zohar.

The Zohar was written in Aramaic. It was published in the thirteenth century by Moses de Leon. He attributed the writing of the book to Rabbi Simeon bar Yohai, who lived in the second century. For thirteen years Rabbi Simeon hid in caves to escape persecution by the Romans. His students sought him out in his hiding places and studied with him at a time when it was forbidden by the Romans to teach or study the Torah. It is believed that during the time that Simeon bar Yohai was hiding, he composed the mystical interpretations of the Bible which came to be called the Zohar.

Simeon bar Yohai's book was given the name Zohar, which means "light," because it sheds light on many aspects of the Torah that would otherwise be hard to understand.

The Zohar explains the Bible in a symbolic manner and finds hidden meanings in simple statements. It has, in addition to Bible commentaries, stories, essays, ethical teachings, and prayers.

Title page of *Tikkunei ha-Zohar,*
Mantua, 1558. Collection.

XXVIII
Shema Yisrael

Deuteronomy 6:1–28:69

After having repeated the story of the giving of the Ten Commandments, Moses declares the other basic teaching of Judaism, the Shema—the oneness of God and Israel's loyalty to Him. The Israelites are then instructed on how they should behave when they are at last in the promised land.

Summary: DEUTERONOMY 6:1–9

Moses said, "These are the laws and rules that the Lord your God has commanded me to teach to you to be followed in the land which you are about to cross into and occupy. Obey them willingly and faithfully that it may go well with you, and that you may increase and prosper in the land which is flowing with milk and honey.

Hear, O Israel!	שְׁמַע יִשְׂרָאֵל
The Lord our God,	יְהֹוָה אֱלֹהֵינוּ
the Lord is one.	יְהֹוָה אֶחָד.

"You shall love the Lord your God with all your soul and with all your might. Take the words which I command you this day to your heart. Teach them to your children. Speak them when you are at home and when you are away, when you lie down and when you rise up. Wrap them as a sign on your hand and as a symbol on your forehead. Write them upon the doorposts of your homes and on your gates.

LEARNING MORE ABOUT:
THE SHEMA

Deuteronomy 6:4 reads, *Shema Yisrael, Adonai Elohenu, Adonai Echad*
—"Hear, O Israel! the Lord our God, the Lord is one." This line has
been called the watchword of our faith, and it is included in all our
prayer services. Many Jews close their eyes while saying the prayer
so that they may concentrate more intensely on the meaning of the
words.

The Shema is one of the most basic beliefs of the Jewish religion,
declaring as it does the oneness of God. It is believed to have been
uttered by Rabbi Akiba, a Jewish martyr, at the moment of his death.
Rabbi Akiba lived in the second century, the Romans ruled Jerusalem.
He was a great teacher and also a great patriot. When Bar Kochba led a
rebellion against the Romans, Rabbi Akiba joined with him. But the
rebellion failed, and the Jews were forbidden by the Romans to study or
teach the Torah. Rabbi Akiba disobeyed and was sentenced to a hor-
rible death. As he was dying, he spoke aloud the words of the Shema.
Since that time, many Jews on the verge of death have tried to make the
words of the Shema their last words.

FOCUS ON:
BIBLICAL SELECTIONS IN THE PRAYERBOOK

The words of the Veahavta as they are found in Deuteronomy and the prayerbook are as follows (the last four lines are from Numbers):

Love the Eternal your God	וְאָהַבְתָּ אֵת יְהֹוָה אֱלֹהֶיךָ
with all your heart, with all your soul,	בְּכָל־לְבָבְךָ וּבְכָל־נַפְשְׁךָ
and with all your might.	וּבְכָל־מְאֹדֶךָ.
The things I ask you to do should be in your heart.	וְהָיוּ הַדְּבָרִים הָאֵלֶּה אֲשֶׁר אָנֹכִי מְצַוְּךָ הַיּוֹם, עַל־לְבָבֶךָ.
Teach them carefully to your children.	וְשִׁנַּנְתָּם לְבָנֶיךָ,
Speak about them in your homes	וְדִבַּרְתָּ בָּם בְּשִׁבְתְּךָ בְּבֵיתֶךָ
and on your way;	וּבְלֶכְתְּךָ בַדֶּרֶךְ,
when you lie down and when you awake.	וּבְשָׁכְבְּךָ וּבְקוּמֶךָ.
Make them as a sign on your hand,	וּקְשַׁרְתָּם לְאוֹת עַל־יָדֶךָ,
and as a symbol on your forehead.	וְהָיוּ לְטֹטָפֹת בֵּין עֵינֶיךָ.
Write them upon the doorposts of your homes	וּכְתַבְתָּם עַל־מְזֻזוֹת בֵּיתֶךָ
and on your gates.	וּבִשְׁעָרֶיךָ.
Be always mindful of My mitzvot and do them.	לְמַעַן תִּזְכְּרוּ וַעֲשִׂיתֶם אֶת־כָּל־מִצְוֹתָי,
Thus will you become holy to your God.	וִהְיִיתֶם קְדוֹשִׁים לֵאלֹהֵיכֶם.
I am the Eternal your God.	אֲנִי יְהֹוָה אֱלֹהֵיכֶם.

"When you are in the land that the Lord promised to your ancestors, be careful that you do not forget the Lord, who freed you from the land of Egypt where you were slaves. Fear only the Lord and worship only Him. Do not follow other gods, lest the anger of God blaze against you and He wipe you off the face of the earth."

COMMENTARIES

From the Midrash

We are commanded to love the Lord with all our soul and all our might. This means that we must strive with all our might to overcome our evil inclinations and to always live by the Lord's commandments.

From the Talmud

Loving the Lord implies more than just fulfilling the letter of the law. It means we must go beyond it and also observe the spirit of the law.

From Rashi

In commanding us to do what is right and good, we are being reminded that we have a moral obligation to go beyond what is legally required of us—that is, to do what is "good" as well as what is "right."

"When the Lord brings you to the land you are about to invade and occupy, and you defeat many nations, you must destroy those nations. Do not make treaties with them. You must not intermarry with them, for they will turn your children away from Me to worship other gods. Tear down their altars, smash their temples, and burn their idols. For you are a people holy to the Lord your God. Of all the peoples on the earth the Lord chose you to be His treasured people.

"Faithfully observe all the commandments that I command you this day, and you will thrive and increase and be able to occupy the land which the Lord promised to your ancestors. Do you remember how you provoked the Lord your God to anger in the wilderness from the day you left Egypt until you reached this place? Now, Israel, what does the Lord your God demand of you? Only to fear Him, to walk only in His path, to love Him and serve Him with all your heart and soul, and to keep His commandments and laws.

"If you faithfully keep all the commandments, the Lord will make you victorious over all these nations. You will conquer nations greater and more numerous than yours. Your territory shall extend from the desert to Lebanon and from the Euphrates River to the Western Sea. No nation shall stand up to you. The Lord your God will make you feared and dreaded in the whole land in which you set foot, as He promised you."

COMMENTARIES

From Rashi

Keeping God's commandments is not without reward, for God rewards those who observe His commandments.

God chose the ancestors of the Israelites from all others to be His people. But the divine choice is not limited to the ancestors. Their descendants, too, are more beloved than other peoples.

LEARNING MORE ABOUT:
TEFILLIN

"Wrap them as a sign on your hand and as a symbol on your forehead."
This commandment has been interpreted as referring to tefillin. Tefillin
are made up of two small boxes containing Torah passages written on
parchment. The boxes are attached to leather bands and are worn by
Orthodox and Conservative Jews on their arm and forehead while reciting Shacharit, the Morning Service.

While many Jews believe that the commandment was meant literal-
ly, others believe that it was meant figuratively. The latter feel that the
passage could be interpreted to mean, "These commandments shall be
for you a reminder, *as if* they were written on your arm and on your
forehead."

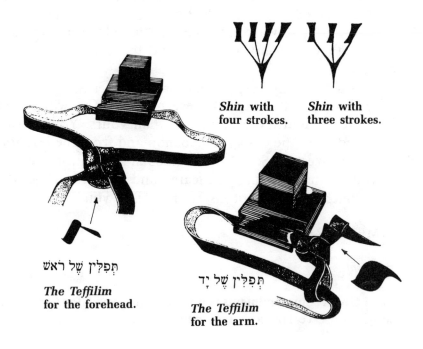

Shin with
four strokes.

Shin with
three strokes.

תְּפִלִין שֶׁל רֹאשׁ

**The Teffilim
for the forehead.**

תְּפִלִין שֶׁל יָד

**The Teffilim
for the arm.**

LEARNING MORE ABOUT:
THE MEZZUZAH

"Write them on the doorposts of your homes and on your gates." This commandment has been interpreted as referring to the mezzuzah. The mezzuzah is a small tubular case of wood, glass, metal, or ceramic which contains inside a small piece of parchment. On the parchment is handwritten the verses from the Shema that are found in Deuteronomy 6:4–9 and 11:13–21.

The mezzuzah is nailed in a slanting position on the upper part of the right doorpost as one enters the house. Some Jews touch the mezzuzah with their fingers and then kiss the fingers every time they enter or leave the house. For many Jews, the mezzuzah is a way of identifying their homes as Jewish homes.

The great Jewish scholar Moses Maimonides wrote that the mezzuzah is a constant reminder of God's unity. He believed that when a person saw the mezzuzah when he entered or left his home, he would be stirred by love of God and would forget unimportant worldly concerns and remember that nothing, except God, lasts forever. This would make him choose the right path.

A mezuzah scroll

191

SOMETHING TO THINK ABOUT

What do you think it means to be "God's Chosen People"? Do most Jews still think of themselves as "more beloved" by God than non-Jews? Is this a concept that has value in our time? Does being the "Chosen People" or "more beloved" place a particular responsibility on Jews?

From Rashi

It is important for a judge to be impartial in judging a case. Even when both parties are first submitting their cases, the judge may not be lenient with one and strict with the other. He should not ask one to stand and the other to be seated, because the one who sees the judge show honor to the other will be so upset that he will not be able to state his case clearly.

From the Talmud

Not only must a judge hand down a decision that is just, but even a compromise must be guided by justice.

FOCUS ON VALUES

Although many of the laws in this chapter involve religious rituals, just as many deal with ethical concepts and with justice. Ethical behavior toward one's fellow-man and the practice of justice have been emphasized as religious obligations in Judaism from the earliest days.

"These are the laws and rules which you must carefully observe in the land that the Lord, the God of your ancestors, is giving to you to possess as long as you live on earth:

"Destroy the altars upon which the nations you conquer worshipped their gods. Do not worship the Lord your God in the manner they do. But look only to the place that the Lord will choose for His place, and there bring burnt-offerings and other sacrifices.

"You may not eat any animals except those that have cleft hoofs and chew the cud. You may eat of all creatures that live in the water only those that have fins and scales. You may eat only clean birds and winged creatures. You may not eat anything that has died a natural death. You shall not boil a kid in its mother's milk.

"You shall set aside every year a tenth part of all the yield of your planting. Then the Levite, who has no hereditary pasture as you have, and the stranger, the orphan, and the widow in your settlement shall come and eat their fill. If there is a needy person among you, do not harden your heart or shut your hand against him. But open your hand and lend him enough for his needs.

"If a fellow Hebrew, man or woman, is sold to you as a slave, he shall serve you for six years and in the seventh you shall set him free. When you set him free, do not let him go empty-handed, but furnish him with food. Remember that you were slaves in the land of Egypt, and the Lord God set you free. But if the slave does not want to leave you, pierce his ear and he will become your slave forever.

"You shall observe the holy days as I have commanded you. Three times a year, on the Feast of Unleavened Bread (Passover), on the Feast of Weeks (Shavuoth), and on the Feast of Booths (Succoth), all your males shall come to the place that I will choose, and each will offer his own gift to the Lord according to the blessings he has received.

"You shall appoint judges and officials for your tribes, and they shall govern the people with justice. They shall show no favoritism and take no bribes.

"If you see someone's ox or sheep which has gone astray, do not ignore it, but take it back to its owner. You shall do the same with anything belonging to another which he loses and you find. You must not remain indifferent.

"A woman must not wear a man's clothing, nor a man a woman's clothing.

"You may not charge interest on loans to your countrymen. But you may charge interest on loans to foreigners.

"When a man takes a bride, he shall not serve in the army for one year, to give happiness to the woman he married.

"You shall not abuse a needy and destitute laborer, whether a countryman or a stranger in one of the communities of your land. You must pay him his wages on the same day before the sun sets, for he is needy and urgently depends on it.

"When you reap the harvest of your fields and overlook a sheaf in the field, do not go back for it. It shall be for the needy.

"If you do not observe these commandments, the Lord your God will scatter you among all the peoples from one end of the earth to the other. Yet even among the nations you shall not find peace, nor shall your foot find a place to rest."

These are the terms of the covenant which the Lord commanded Moses to make with the Israelites in the land of Moab in addition to the covenant that He made with them at Horeb (Sinai).

COMMENTARIES

From the Midrash

The commandments of the Torah and the soul of a person can be compared to a light. God said to man, "My light is in your hand, and your light is in My hand. If you guard My light, I will guard your light. But if you extinguish My light, then I will also extinguish your light."

SOMETHING TO THINK ABOUT

What do you think this commentary means? What is "God's light"? What is "mankind's light"?

XXIX

Moses' Farewell

Deuteronomy 29:1−32:52

Moses calls together the Children of Israel for the last time in his lifetime and charges them to love and obey God. He then appoints Joshua as his successor and gives final instructions to him and the Levites.

As Moses prepares for death, he sings a hymn of praise to God's glory.

Summary: DEUTERONOMY 29:1−30:20

Moses called all Israel and said to them, "You have seen all that the Lord did before your eyes in the land of Egypt. He led you through the wilderness for forty years and took care of your needs. And when you reached this place and your enemies engaged you in battle, we defeated them and took their land. Therefore observe carefully all the terms of this covenant so that you may succeed in all that you do.

"You are standing this day, all of you, before the Lord your God—your tribal heads, your elders and officials, your children, your wives, even the stranger within your camp, from the wood-chopper to the waterdrawer—to enter into the covenant with the Lord your God, as He swore to your ancestors. I make this covenant not with you alone, but with those who are standing here this day before the Lord your God, and with those who are not with us here this day.

196

"I set before you this day life and goodness, death and evil. Love the Lord your God, and walk in His ways and keep His commandments, His laws, and His rules, that the Lord your God may bless you in the land which you are about to invade and occupy. I have put before you life and death, blessing and curse. Choose life by loving the Lord your God, and obeying His commandments."

COMMENTARIES

From the Midrash

God said to the Children of Israel, "My children, if the words of the Torah are near to you, then you will be near to Me."

Although it is a sacred obligation to learn the entire Torah so that we may obey its commandments, it is foolish to try to learn it all at once. There is the danger that in doing so we will become so discouraged by the impossible task that we will give up altogether. It is far better to study a little every day.

After Moses had spoken these things to all Israel, he said to them, "I am now 120 years old. I can no longer be active. And God has said to me, 'You shall not go across this Jordan.' "

Then Moses called up Joshua and said to him before all Israel, "Be strong and of good courage, because you shall go with this people into the land that the Lord swore to their ancestors to give them. The Lord Himself shall go before you. He will not fail you or forsake you. Do not be afraid!"

Then Moses wrote down this teaching and gave it to the priests, the sons of Levi, who carried the Ark of the Covenant, and to all the elders of Israel. And Moses instructed them to read the law and teach it to all the people of the community so that they might learn to observe carefully every word of this teaching.

When he had finished, the Lord said to Moses, "The time is coming close for you to die. You are soon to lie with your ancestors."

COMMENTARIES

From the Midrash

When it was time for Moses to die, he prayed to God to be spared from death. But God answered, "No person can live and not die. Even great men like Abraham, Isaac, and Jacob had to die when their time came. So, too, must you die, even though there was never another like you who spoke to Me face to face." So Moses pepared to die.

At first Moses did not want to die. But after Joshua was appointed to succeed him, the two men went into the Tabernacle. There a cloud separated them, and the Lord spoke only to Joshua. Moses could no longer hear God's voice, and he envied Joshua. It was then that he was ready to die, for it is better to die a hundred times than to experience even one moment of envy.

Summary: DEUTERONOMY 31:30–32:52

Then Moses recited the words of this poem to the very end, in the hearing of the whole congregation of Israel:

> Give ear, O heavens, let me speak,
> Let the earth hear the words I utter.
> Remember the days of old.
> Consider the years of ages past.
> You neglected the Lord who created you,
> Forgot the God who brought you forth.
> The Lord saw and was angry.
> He said: I will hide My face from My sons and daughters,
> And see how well they do in the end.
> For they are treacherous—children with no loyalty in them.
> But the Lord will judge His people.
> See then that I am He.
> There is no other God beside Me.
> I ordain death and give life.
> None can deliver from My hand.

When Moses finished reciting all these words to all Israel, he said to them, "Take to heart all the words with which I have warned you this day. Tell them to your children that you may observe carefully all the words of this teaching. For this is not a small thing for you. It is our very life. Through it you shall long endure on the land which you are to occupy upon crossing the Jordan."

That very day the Lord spoke to Moses, "Climb to the top of Mount Nebo and view the land of Canaan which I am giving to the Israelites as their possession. You will die on the mountain and be gathered to your ancestors. For you broke faith with Me at the waters of Meribath-Kadesh in the Wilderness of Zin. You may view the land from a distance, but you shall not enter into the land that I am giving to the Israelite people."

COMMENTARIES

From Rashi

Moses' farewell song had both words of warning and words of consolation, so that the Israelites would know that if they turned against God they would face calamity, but if they obeyed God and His commandments God would console and comfort them.

XXX

The Death of Moses

Deuteronomy 33:1—34:12

Moses blesses the Children of Israel and prays for the well-being of each of the tribes. God then shows him the promised land for the last time and Moses dies.

Summary: DEUTERONOMY 33:1—29

This is the blessing with which Moses, the man of God, blessed the Israelites before he died:

May the children of Reuben live and not die,
And may they be numbered.

Hear, O Lord, the voice of Judah,
And help him against his enemies.

Bless Levi and favor his works;
Let his enemies arise no more.

Benjamin, beloved of God,
May the Lord rest securely beside him and protect him.

May Joseph's land be blessed
With the bounty and fullness of the earth.

And bless also Ephraim and Manasseh
With strength and prosperity.

Rejoice, O Zebulun,
In your travels.

And be happy, Issachar,
In your tents.

Blessed is the Lord, who makes Gad strong
And enlarges his territory.

And makes Dan like a young lion
Who leaps forth from Bashan.

May Naphtali, full of the Lord's blessing,
Take possession of the west and the south.

And may the sons of Asher be blessed
And be secure all their lives.

O happy Israel! Who is like you?
A people delivered by the Lord.
Your enemies shall fall before you,
And you shall be victorious over them.

FOCUS ON:
BIBLICAL SELECTIONS IN THE PRAYERBOOK

The following quotation from Deuteronomy 33 is in the Morning Service (Shacharit).

This is the Torah that Moses
  commanded us.

תּוֹרָה צִוָּה לָנוּ מֹשֶׁה,

It is the heritage of the congregation of Jacob.

מוֹרָשָׁה קְהִלַּת יַעֲקֹב.

COMMENTARIES

From the Midrash

When God came to take Moses at the time that he was to die, Moses said, "All these years I have spoken harshly to the Children of Israel and criticized them for their faults. Now that I am about to die, I would like to bless them." And Moses blessed them according to their tribes.

Moses called the tribe of Benjamin the "beloved of God" because in the future the Holy City of Jerusalem would be located in its territory.

Then Moses went up from Moab to Mount Nebo, and the Lord showed him the whole land,

and the Lord said to him:	וַיֹּאמֶר יְהֹוָה אֵלָיו
"This is the land	זֹאת הָאָרֶץ אֲשֶׁר
which I swore to Abraham, Isaac, and Jacob:	נִשְׁבַּעְתִּי לְאַבְרָהָם לְיִצְחָק וּלְיַעֲקֹב
I will give it to your descendants.	לֵאמֹר לְזַרְעֲךָ אֶתְּנֶנָּה
I have let you see it with your own eyes,	הֶרְאִיתִיךָ בְעֵינֶיךָ
but you shall not cross there."	וְשָׁמָּה לֹא תַעֲבֹר:

So Moses, the servant of the Lord, died there, in the land of Moab, at the command of the Lord. He buried him in the valley in the land of Moab, and no one knows his burial place to this day. Moses was 120 years old when he died. His eyes were undimmed, and he was as strong as in his youth. And the Israelites cried for Moses and mourned him for thirty days.

Joshua the son of Nun was filled with the spirit of wisdom because Moses had laid his hands on him. And the Israelites listened to him, doing as the Lord had commanded them.

But never again did there arise in Israel a prophet like Moses who knew the Lord face to face.